# THE HEADHUNTER'S EDGE

JEFFREY E. CHRISTIAN

# The Headhunter's Edge

Random House / New York

Copyright © 2002 by Jeffrey E. Christian

All rights reserved under International and Pan-American Copyright Con-
ventions. Published in the United States by Random House, Inc., New York,
and simultaneously in Canada by Random House of Canada Limited,
Toronto.

RANDOM HOUSE and colophon are registered trademarks of Random House,
Inc.

Library of Congress Cataloging-in-Publication Data

Christian, Jeffrey E.
The headhunter's edge
p.        cm.
ISBN 0-375-50543-1
1. Executives—Recruiting—United States.    2. Chief executive officers—
Recruiting—United States.    3. Employees—Recruiting—United States.
4. Employee selection—United States.    I. Title.
HF5549.5.R44 C456 2002        658.4'0711—dc21        2001041880

Random House website address: www.atrandom.com

Manufactured in the United States of America on acid-free paper

2  4  6  8  9  7  5  3

First Edition

This title is available at a discount when ordering 25 or more copies for sales,
promotions, or corporate use. Special editions, including personalized cov-
ers, excerpts, and corporate imprints can be created when purchasing in
large quantities. For more information, please call (800) 800-3246 or e-mail
*specialmarkets@randomhouse.com*.

*To my family, especially Lori, the most loving—and talented—wife and mother of my children I could ever have hoped for*

# CONTENTS

## PART III
### CONCLUSION

# THE TALENT PRINCIPLE

CHAPTER 1

*It's a Talent Economy*

Not long ago, I set up a meeting between a CEO with a big job to fill and a talented manager I had interviewed who seemed a perfect match. I made arrangements for the candidate to fly in for a meeting with the CEO at his office. Simple, right?

Not when the CEO refused to pay for a limo to transport him to the company's offices. The candidate ended up taking a taxi—and getting lost. And as if that weren't bad enough, when he finally arrived at the company's offices, he had the pleasure of sitting and waiting, and waiting, in the reception area. A half hour past the appointed time, and with no sign of the CEO, the job candidate rose from his chair in disgust and walked out the door. And thus my client lost the one person available who was, in the opinion of his high-priced search professional, perfect for the job. Why did my client lose Mr. Right? Because like too many CEOs—and general managers of engineering, vice presidents of sales, directors of marketing, and managers of *whatever* with hiring responsibility—he had not committed his brain, his heart, and the future of his company to what I call the Talent Principle:

*The company with the best people thrives.*

What about the best product? What about marketing or sales? Strategic thinking? What about all those wizard business models coming out of the B-schools? They do not drive business. Talent does. In fact, there is no such thing as "sales" or "marketing" or even "product" without people. If, for example, you have a marketing problem in your company, then my advice would be to hire a more talented person to run the marketing department. The real art of building a successful company is to bring together so much talent that no one would want to work anyplace else, and that those who do will want to be part of your winning team. I would even go so far as to argue that you can build a major career in business simply by surrounding yourself with the best people you can find. Talent will draw more talent. It is the kind of virtuous circle you want in your career and your company at every level, from CEO right down the pyramid. If you are at the beginning of your career, attach yourself to the best people in your company; find mentors. If you're already in a position of power, recruit the best people you can possibly find and keep them at your side. If you hire talented lieutenants, they'll tell you what to do. All you have to do is listen. It's that simple.

Finding all those talented people is a bit more difficult. So is interviewing for talent and persuading the best people that their future is with you. The most difficult challenge of all can be to keep the great talent you have from accepting another job offer. How do you get the best people and keep them? How do you create a career so that you will be identified as "talent"?

*You have to learn to think like a headhunter.*

That is the goal of this book. If I can help some of the most successful companies in the world find the smartest, most creative, and hardest-working talent available, then I think I can help you, too. In 1980, I founded Christian & Timbers, the first search firm specializing in information technology. Our work has affected thousands of companies, ranging from such Fortune 50 legends as IBM, Microsoft, and Apple Computer to such Internet and e-commerce pioneers as Lycos, Netscape, Cisco, Amazon, and Yahoo. When Hewlett-Packard's chairman, president, and CEO, Lew Platt, decided in 1999 to replace himself, HP chose us to do the search. I brought them one of Lucent's rising stars, Carly Fiorina, who as HP's new president and CEO has injected new life into one of America's great companies. Today, Christian & Timbers is one of the top ten search firms in the nation, with thirty partners and fourteen offices in the United States, Canada, and Europe. It has been a great ride, fueled partly, of course, by one of the most impressive economic booms in U.S. history. But my company—and my competitors in the executive search industry—have also benefited from what I believe is one of the most profound constants in the marketplace:

*There is always a talent shortage.*

At no time in history has this been truer than today, when every top company in the world finds itself competing for talent. Forget the hype about the "New Economy," the "Internet Economy," and the "New New Economy." You cannot even be distracted by an economy in recession. We are operating in a *Talent Economy*, where only companies who hire the best people will thrive.

## THE WORLD WAR FOR TALENT

In the 1960s only 9 percent of new chief executives came from outside the company; today upwards of 40 percent of new CEOs are recruited from elsewhere. Meanwhile, the pool of executives qualified for top management positions has actually been drying up. In 1999, *Fortune* reported that Silicon Valley "has been short of talent for a decade or more, but there's evidence the problem is getting more desperate and far-reaching than ever." The magazine pointed to five hundred vacant high-tech CEO positions in the Valley alone and cited a study that concluded that so many empty top jobs cost companies in the area upwards of $4 billion annually in lost opportunities and productivity. Even after the Internet bubble burst on Wall Street in April 2000 and the NASDAQ lost 65 percent of its value, the talent crunch persisted. High-flying companies had suddenly crashed to earth. Those that were still alive needed intensive care. But the kind of leader who can revive sick companies is rare in the best of times. Suddenly, "turnaround CEOs" were in high demand. Early-stage companies that had been looking for CEOs now wanted COOs with proven skills in running a business day-to-day whom they could groom for the CEO spot. Top companies surveyed the wreckage of the dot-coms and snapped up the best managers, many of whom found themselves hotly pursued by more traditional firms desperate for Internet expertise as well as what wisdom they might have picked up watching their start-ups or early-stage companies imploding. New companies reacquainting themselves with the old saying in business that "Nothing happens until something is sold" were searching for vice presidents of sales. Every company seemed eager to cut costs and wanted an experienced chief financial officer to do it. Particularly hot were CFOs with international experience. Technology is now a global business, and U.S. companies with the financial talent to manage money worldwide will have an edge on their competition. In interviews with one hundred senior managers of Fortune 500 and venture-backed companies about their future hiring needs, Christian & Timbers also found out that with Europeans discovering the joys of instant messaging and Americans trying to download the entire Internet into the palm of their hand, the need for management talent in the wireless space had not abated. Fiber optics companies still racing to create the perfect fiber optics switch were scouting for talented engineers—and would be for the next decade, the best guess for when the new networks would be in place. Software programmers are still in demand, and there remains a shortage of good computer engineers.

Nor has the talent crunch been limited only to technology. By mid-2000, the requests for top executives in the biotechnology sector were already up 300 percent over the previous year, according to search-industry surveys; analysts were predicting the biotech business to grow annually by 20 percent over the next decade. Healthcare is wide-open for talent. Hospitals report one of the highest rates of job growth in the nation. According to the Bureau of Labor Statistics, nurses, health technicians, and researchers are among the top five professions with the largest job growth and persistent need—right up there with the high demand for computer scientists. The aging of the Baby Boomers is likely to keep the employment opportunities in the healthcare and life sciences professions recession-proof. The number of law graduates has not budged in recent years, which has put smart, young lawyers at a premium. (Our hiring study in the first quarter of 2001 revealed a major shortage of bankruptcy attorneys—not surprising considering that the economy was on the verge of recession.) Financial services companies are also competing for young talent. Even major consulting companies such as McKinsey, Bain, and Booz-Allen, which used to have their pick of the best graduates of the best business schools, have had to sweeten compensation for young associates, as well as for partners who find themselves tempted to fill some of those CEO vacancies around the country.

Today's top executives must be more qualified than ever before. Leaders in the biotech industry, for example, have traditionally had scientific backgrounds, M.D.s, and Ph.D.s. But to make it at the top of biotech in the future will require an understanding of the technology driving scientific development, along with regulatory policy, not to mention the ability to convince venture-capital firms and other investors that you have the skills to take a start-up or early-stage company to $500 million in a flash. Executives with all these skills are rare. Even the utility sector is scrambling for talent. Deprived of their captive markets by deregulation, utilities have been forced to consolidate and restructure. Suddenly, they have to become real businesses and compete for customers, which requires the kind of marketing talent that utility executives never needed. Sixty-five percent of recent hires came from outside the utilities industry—the same people every other industry in America is after.

U.S. companies are not alone in their scramble for talent. As I write, the business press is full of stories about how the talent crunch has spread abroad. In Europe, where opposition to immigration has been a divisive political issue for decades, governments are trying to figure out how to bring in more workers to fill jobs. In March 2000, the British Chancellor of the Exchequer proposed to relax rules on hiring skilled foreign nationals. The German leader, Gerhard Schroeder, provoked a national debate when he proposed lifting visa restrictions to allow software experts from India and elsewhere to work in Germany. Young Europeans, savvier than ever about managing their careers, know that mobility works to their advantage. Why limit a career to your native country when corporations throughout the European Union are scouting for the best people? To keep their talent, European corporations are employing methods that only a few years ago were viewed as evidence of non-European (read "American") greediness—namely, stock options. At stake, argue European analysts, is the continent's economic growth. According to a 2000 study commissioned by Microsoft Europe and published by International Data Corporation, European demand for skilled professionals in telecommunications and computers over the next three years could outstrip supply by 13 percent.

Ireland is already literally begging for talent. In the late 1980s, the tiny country of 3.6 million was in an economic depression with 18 percent unemployment and 20 percent inflation, watching 45,000 people a year emigrate to find work. In 2001–2002, Ireland was boasting the fastest-growing economy in Europe (and the seventh most competitive in the world). Desperate for talent at every level of business, the Irish government has created a "Department for Enterprise, Trade and Employment," which during the past year has held job fairs in Prague, Berlin, Hannover, Birmingham, Liverpool, Bombay, Newfoundland, Moscow, and New York.

It seems that every business in the world needs talent. Yesterday. And the reason is very simple: demographics. As the fabled Baby Boomers move into the final stage of their careers, there are simply fewer twenty-five-to-thirty-nine-year-olds to replace them. While the U.S. economy has doubled over the past thirty years, the birth-rate has dropped by 24 percent. Assuming that the economy grows a mere 2 percent a year for the next fifteen years, the international search firm Spencer Stuart has projected that the demand for man-agers will increase by a third, while Americans in the prime of their careers—thirty-five to forty-four years old—will decline by 15 percent. The demographics are no more promising in the rest of the world. Several social factors are also in play worldwide: managers are moving from company to company more often; two-career couples are less eager to move to another part of the coun-try (or world); and young managers are more impatient about moving up the ladder. That is why the leaders of the best compa-nies in the world and the venture capitalists investing in the best companies of the future spend most of their time recruiting talent. "In a knowledge-based world economy, the most competitive nations have to be attractive to the best people," says Stephane Garelli, the director of the World Competitiveness Project 2001, an organization that rates the economies of forty-nine countries, using data from international and regional organizations. (The United States remains the number-one most competitive country.)

# IF JACK WELCH WAS OBSESSED WITH TALENT, SHOULDN'T YOU BE, TOO?

The most exceptional business leaders seem to have an appreciation for the power of talent built into their DNA. I would argue that at any time in history the best companies have been the ones most focused on talent. Why did General Motors or Ford survive while Studebaker and American Motors bite the dust? Talent. Why did John D. Rockefeller's Standard Oil monopolize the energy business rather than the thousands of other oil refineries around the country? Talent. Why were IBM and General Electric legendary American companies before Jack Welch and Lew Gerstner were even born? Talent.

Neither Ford nor Rockefeller—nor the founders of IBM and GE—needed any studies to convince them of the importance of talent. But many of my clients need to be persuaded. Finally, studies of the effects of talent on a company's productivity and profits have been done, and—surprise—they have confirmed what the great business leaders already know in their gut: the difference between making things happen in the marketplace and fading into oblivion is talent. After spending three years researching the relationship between talent management and financial performance in fifty-six large and successful companies—thirty-five of them with over $1 billion in revenue—McKinsey & Company found that talented managers generated "enormous value" for their employers. According to the McKinsey research, a company's best performers—what McKinsey calls the "A players"—are 50 to 100 percent more productive than average performers or underperformers. Comparing performance in three companies in different industries, the study found that the best account executives in a financial services company grew revenue by 52 percent, top service center managers in an industrial services company grew profits 82 percent, and the most successful plant managers in a manufacturing company increased revenue an eye-popping 129 percent. The productivity of average or underperformers in those same companies was barely noticeable. McKinsey recommended paying to keep top performers. "Even if you pay an 'A' player 40 percent more to retain him/her," the report concluded, "your investment yields a 300 percent one year return on investment."

Bill Gates and Jack Welch did not need to commission McKinsey to tell them that talent pays. While competitors are shopping for a new Gulfstream jet or romancing the writer from *Fortune*, Bill Gates is on a recruiting trip. From the beginning, he has relied on a small group of engineers to help him design Microsoft's products and the strategies to get them to market. Gates realized that if he was going to compete with Apple, he would have to hire programmers as good as Apple's. They didn't exist, so he hired away some of Apple's best people. Twenty years ago, Gates lured away the computer visionary Charles Simonyi, who helped Microsoft bury the competition. As the key members of his brain trust have burnt out or departed to enjoy the millions they made in Microsoft stock, Gates was always on the prowl for replacements. In 1992, he flew to New York to recruit Craig Mundie, a computer scientist who had developed the operating system for a Data General minicomputer. Two years later, he signed on Paul Flessner, another computer scientist who had managed large corporate computer systems and who had been an outspoken critic of Microsoft's software. Mundie ended up running the company's consumer products division, developing the Windows CE operating system, the Handheld, Pocket, and Auto PCs; he was also involved in the acquisition of WebTV. Mundie is now working full time as Gates's prime strategist for reinventing the company. Flessner has refocused the company on quality control, transforming Microsoft's fifty-million-dollar database division into a billion-dollar operation. As Flessner quickly won a reputation as a manager who not only knew what he was doing but was also brilliant at motivating a diverse team of computer scientists with egos bigger than their stock options, software developers quit IBM and Tandem to work for him. I myself have been chewed up by the Gates recruiting machine. In 1997, when my company was in the middle of a search for Borland Software, Microsoft offered Borland's top two programmers million-dollar signing bonuses plus vast stock options to move to Microsoft's headquarters in Redmond, Washington.

Gates has been known to spend 50 percent of his time getting on a plane to interview and recruit talent. Jack Welch said he devoted more than 50 percent of his time to building the best management teams throughout the GE empire. "Our true 'core competency' today is not manufacturing or services, but the global recruiting and nurturing of the world's best people," Welch said in the GE annual report just before he retired. "By finding, challenging and rewarding these people, by freeing them from bureaucracy, by giving them all the resources they need—and by simply getting out of their way—we have seen them make us better every year."

No wonder GE was number one on *Fortune*'s list of "most admired" companies in the world. Microsoft was number three. The number two company was Cisco, whose CEO, John Chambers, has dealt with the talent threat from competitors in the same way John D. Rockefeller outmaneuvered competing oil refineries: he buys their companies—twenty-two alone in 2000. "When we acquire, all I'm acquiring is people and next-generation products," Chambers has explained. "I pay between $20,000 and $20 million per employee for a firm. If I lose those people, I'm in trouble." The toughest companies for headhunters to recruit from in the 1990s? Cisco, Microsoft, and GE. I would also add Intel, Wal-Mart, and Dell—numbers four, five, and seven on *Fortune*'s Global Most Admired list. It is also worth noting that the primary criterion for qualifying for the *Fortune*'s list was "quality of management." (Another main measure was "ability to attract, develop, and retain talent.")

## THE VCs BET THEIR MONEY ON—TALENT

Ten years ago, when venture capitalists raised money for what they were betting was a $10 million company, they would expect to take it public at $100 million in seven years and after four consecutive quarters of profitability. That was the formula. A founding entrepreneur had the opportunity to run the company for years before the VCs would step in and demand new leadership. In the late 1990s, however, as the Internet sped up the way everyone did business, the values of companies also rose faster. Year-old companies with no profits were routinely going public. More astounding, the venture guys began *expecting* that they could get that $100 million valuation, take the company public, and then expect a billion-dollar cap—within twelve months of start-up! With that kind of money at stake, it's no wonder that the first thing the VCs did after putting together the pre-IPO financing of a new company was to call their headhunter.

John Doerr, one of the world's top venture capitalists and a general partner with Kleiner, Perkins, Caufield & Byers, the VC firm founded in 1972 that helped finance Silicon Valley, has said he spends "120 percent" of his time recruiting the leadership for the companies he bankrolls. Working with Doerr, I have called him on his cell phone on a Sunday morning, catching him on the church steps. He even sounded happy to hear from me. Venture capitalists no longer see themselves as mere money guys but as "company builders." They not only serve on the boards of the firms they invest in, they are also inclined to handpick the CEO and top management and then stay involved in the company as an informal consultant.

*Red Herring* magazine recently put Vinod Khosla on the cover with the banner "The No. 1 VC on the Planet." One of the founders of Sun Microsystems and now a general partner at Kleiner, Perkins, the forty-six-year-old Khosla has helped create forty companies that have produced a total market value of $150 billion. In 1996, he put together a small optical networking company that made a box the size of a microwave that could transfer four million telephone calls per second from old copper lines onto speedier fiber-optic cables. Khosla invested $8 million for a 30 percent stake of the company. Three years later, Cisco bought the company—Cerent—for $8 *billion,* increasing Khosla's investment 300 times, to $2.4 billion! The success of Juniper Networks, the Internet router company he also helped launch, quickly turned Khosla's $3 million investment into $4.3 billion. Only John Doerr has created more multibillion-dollar companies. According to *Red Herring,* "many believe Mr. Khosla is to venture capital what Michael Jordan is to basketball or Gary Kasparov to chess." Count me among Vinod Khosla's biggest fans. But the *Red Herring* cover story neglected what I think is one of the main reasons for Khosla's success: He's the best recruiter of talent I have ever seen. Khosla not only invests in companies, he also sits in as the interim CEO and works flat out to find the right person to run the company along with a talented management team. Recently, I have worked on three CEO searches with him, and I was amazed by his commitment to finding the right person for the job. "The right leadership and 'gene pool' is the most important thing to a company's success," Khosla explained. "The CEO's thirst for talent and his salesmanship in recruiting talent and building teams are key to determining the future of the company." Vinod Khosla is such a natural-born headhunter that even if I could bottle his skills and feed them to the best recruiters in my firm, I doubt I could create his equal.

Fortunately, venture firms can't clone Khosla (or Doerr), which means they have to hire people like me to help them recruit talent. Some firms have gone one step further. Two years after the venture-capital firm Benchmark set up shop in 1995 in an office park on Sand Hill Road in Menlo Park, California, the VC row of Silicon Valley, one of its first decisions was to offer a partnership to David Beirne, the young founder of Ramsey Beirne, a New York search firm that Bill Gates liked to work with. When John Doerr (Kleiner, Perkins is also a resident of Sand Hill Road) heard that the new kids on the block had made an offer to Beirne, he made a counteroffer. Beirne decided that he would have more influence at an upstart firm, which, as it happened, made its first investment in a start-up on-line auction company called eBay. The company grew, went public, and the rest is Wall Street history. Within two years, eBay was valued at more than $21 billion. Benchmark's $6.7 million investment had increased by 100,000 percent, making it Silicon Valley's best-performing venture investment ever. Such astounding successes require great and revolutionary ideas. Of course. But no great idea can become a great company without finding what Beirne likes to call "The Guy"—an A manager who hires A managers. (Let me quickly add that today "The Guy" is often a woman. Talent is not limited by gender.)

The difference in companies is always related to talent. As a headhunter, my primary measure for a great manager is his or her attitude toward hiring talent. I agree absolutely with something Vinod Khosla told me recently. "In most situations," he said, "I would pick a person who has a thirst for great teams, is a great recruiter and a team leader over someone with great financial or marketing skills, industry knowledge or deep technical strength." One measure of how important A players are is what happens to companies that lose their talent.

## LOSE YOUR TALENT—LOSE YOUR EDGE

That was certainly the story of the Digital Equipment Corporation, which in the early 1980s was the second-largest computer company in the world and poised to grab a huge share of the new personal computer business. Trouble was, Digital's founder and CEO, Ken Olsen, didn't believe PCs had a future. "Personal computers?" he once said. "They're great—and everyone will have one in their closet." His top managers begged to disagree, but Olsen was the boss (and not one inclined to share power). So Digital's talent began walking out the door—to help Apple, Microsoft, and Dell change the world. Digital soon became a formerly great American company. And when too many of Apple's most creative minds and managers went to Dell, Compaq, and Microsoft, so did a large pile of that company's revenue (and shareholder value). Motorola began to leak talent, and stalled; so did Xerox. But when you analyze the great companies, the perennial best companies in America, you will notice that their top managers have spent most of their careers there. Good people never left IBM; same with Intel, Cisco, and Microsoft. The three men in line for Jack Welch's job as CEO of General Electric had been with the company for eighteen years each, having risen through the ranks to run several major divisions of GE.

So why do so many CEOs and other top managers with hiring responsibility act as if the best talent in the world is eager to be left sitting in their reception areas? One main reason: they do not understand how important talent is to building their businesses, or even their own careers. I have made it my mission in life to convince corporate executives and their boards how crucial talent is to success in business, and they tend to nod: yes, of course, they understand my point—talent, talent, talent. They then proceed to high-hat the very people they should be romancing and end up hiring someone for all the wrong reasons. Traditionally, managers at every level have left hiring up to underlings or their brother-in-law in a cubicle downstairs labeled "Personnel." These days the department has the more New Agey title of "Human Resources," but for too many companies, their commitment to talent has not changed. In 1999, Watson Wyatt, an employment consulting firm, surveyed 551 large U.S. companies and found that 45 percent had no formal recruiting strategy. In my experience, that's an optimistic number. Such a careless attitude toward talent among so many CEOs is the most frustrating part of my job. But I am inclined to sympathize—mainly because I used to be just as slapdash about my own company's hiring practices. I spent fifteen years trying to build my own recruiting firm without spending enough time recruiting my own talent. Like most entrepreneurs, I was spending 100 percent of my time (and 150 percent of my marriage) trying to keep my company above water, trying to meet the payroll. Even when things were going great, I was working nonstop to boost the company to the next level. Who had time to fly off and romance new employees? But I kept running into one obstacle after another—until I realized that the solution to every one of those problems was people. I am now part of a very successful company. I think I can help you to become more successful—not because I did everything right but because I did everything wrong when it came to hiring and creating a productive working environment. If my infant company had been a real baby, I would have been indicted for child neglect.

## THE EDUCATION OF A HEADHUNTER

I was twenty-three years old and engaged to be married, and while my future in-laws seemed to be well disposed toward me, they certainly had reason to be concerned: I was unemployed. Nor did I have a sterling résumé. In fact, my formal education was stalled in the eighth grade. It's not that I lacked ambition; it's just that my ambition during the 1970s was to be different, and at that I was a success, to my parent's dismay. I gave up meat, I practiced Tai Chi, I learned to meditate. I was also inclined to big ideas—a bit bigger, perhaps, than I was ready to chew. I had already tried to start a natural food business. (The right idea at the right time, but definitely the wrong location. No traffic. Very depressing. Folded.) By my late teens, I managed to take some courses and get into nearby

John Carroll University. But, for financial reasons, I also had to work. I sold mopeds, and I sold airtime for a local radio station. I had just spent the summer working for an uncle in the aluminum foil conversion business. I had even considered being an actor.

On the verge of marriage, I was finally ready to get serious about the future. I wanted to be an entrepreneur. My plan was to work for my father, who owned a small employment agency. I had this idea of franchising his company and growing it to a thousand offices around the country. Trouble was, my dad didn't like that idea. He didn't even like the idea of me working for him, at least not right away. He thought that if I was serious (or maybe to prove that I was) I should go to work for a competitor or a recruiting firm and learn the employment business.

In 1979, I got a job at R.F. Timbers & Company, a Cleveland search firm that worked both on a retainer and a contingency basis. I shared an office not much bigger than a closet with a guy named Max who drank fifty cups of coffee a day and smoked about a hundred cigarettes. My boss, Dick Timbers, liked people to specialize—someone to handle recruiting for manufacturing firms, someone else to cover financial services or retail, and so on. I was given chemicals and plastics. I was also given a big notepad, the Yellow Pages, and a telephone. That was it. No training program, no manual, no mentor. And I certainly had no network of executives—in *any* business, never mind plastics or chemicals.

I did what I had to do. I grabbed the phone and started calling around. I had never been particularly shy. As a middle-class midwestern kid, I had grown up around a wide range of people, from the business types moving through my father's office, where I helped out on Saturdays, to the actors, artists, writers, social activists, and various hangers-on in the bohemian circles my mother traveled in. She worked for a Cleveland newspaper and was the assistant editor of World Publishing Company, but her passion was the theater. She directed and acted in regional theater, and as a little kid I hung around backstage, taking in the sights. I met actors, jazz musicians, motorcycle guys, cops, poets, rock-and-rollers, Black Nationalists, and civil rights activists. I remember going with my mother to a "Ban the Bomb" demonstration when I was in kindergarten. I became a people-watcher, and there was plenty to watch—and watch out for. There were people who enjoyed being around the passion of artists, actors, and civil rights activists, and then there were those whose passion was ripping them off. My mother was a beautiful and compassionate woman, but she didn't always know the difference between the good guys and the scam artists. I quickly learned to distinguish between the two. As distracted as I might have been from my formal studies, I was a devoted student of people, and that turned out to be invaluable training for a young, ambitious headhunter.

I connected easily with people, even over the phone, and my BS-detector was already operating at high frequency. I, too, tended to get passionate about whatever project I was working on, and I quickly discovered that people responded favorably to enthusiasm. And I did a lot of reading. I plowed through every book I could find on sales, marketing, and leadership. I soon realized that companies were always looking for new people and new solutions to their problems. Any headhunter who could listen to the client, provide insight about the company to the candidate, push back on both sides, and close the deal could make an impression. I started hunting for an edge on the competition. My father had specialized in recruiting for the insurance industry, turning himself into an expert on benefits and compensation. What could my expertise be? I found it in a magazine reference to recent advances in "robotics." My mind began racing: maybe this was the birth of a new industry—intelligent robots building things. And who better to staff it than an avid science-fiction reader who already knew all about robots from books by Isaac Asimov? I began researching the automation business. I telephoned all the major players, who, I was surprised to find out, had been waiting for someone like me to call and help fill the vacancies they had at their companies.

I was having a lot of fun, and making some money; but there was one problem: I had to decide whether to stay in college and finish my degree or become the entrepreneur I had dreamed about being. I persuaded Dick Timbers to let me spin myself off into a separate operation with his financial backing and build the first firm to specialize in filling positions in the technology industry, which I discovered was remarkably underserviced by the big search firms. Unlike Timbers, I didn't think a search company could be credible working for some clients on a contingency basis and others on retainer; besides, the major firms did retained work, and I was looking to be major. Within eight months, I bought him out and in 1980 launched Christian & Timbers—myself, another headhunter, and an administrative assistant.

I was the greenest CEO in America. But I was also making money, thanks to a booming economy. While the Age of Robotics did not happen, the personal computer revolution did, and we had established ourselves as experts in technology. Computer and related businesses hired us to find them senior engineers, project managers, and directors—fast. To help me handle the increased workload, I began hiring people who were no more experienced as headhunters or in technology than their CEO, who was now pushing twenty-five. If someone in a decent suit with a flash of intelli-

# WELCOME TO WATERWAY
www.waterway.com
00008987323

| Descr. | qty | amount |
|--------|-----|--------|
| T  WHOLE THING | 1 | 30.00 |

| | | |
|---|---|---|
| Sub Total | | 30.00 |
| Tax | | 2.03 |
| TOTAL | | 32.03 |
| CASH $ | | 50.00 |
| Change $ | | -17.97 |

## 24 HOUR
## RAIN GUARANTEE

REG# 0003 CSH# 008 DR# 01  TRAN# 31933
10/26/14  10:05:29          ST# AB123

gence in his eyes walked in looking for a job, I hired him. It didn't seem to matter. We were not exactly *searching* for the next Steve Jobs. Sure, we were doing retained work, but at the low end. Our clients had positions to be filled, and all we were required to do was to find someone who had done the job before or had the appropriate academic credentials. We left the serious interviewing and evaluating of candidates to the company, which was a good thing because my colleagues and I had no idea what made a good senior engineer or project manager, never mind a great one. We soon had a staff of twenty-five. Christian & Timbers was thriving.

But I had a lot to learn. Intellectually, I knew that having smart, talented people around me was crucial to proving to clients that we were ready to do bigger searches. Watching my mother work in the theater had alerted me to the difference talent could make in a play; and my father had advised me to find the best people possible for my clients, and various clients told me that hiring talented people was key to their growth. Practically, however, I was working like a coal miner to meet the payroll every week. Even if I could devote more time to recruiting for my own company, I was not really sure what kind of people I should be looking for. What was the measure of a good headhunter? I had no idea. I wasn't even sure how talented *I* was. Occasionally I would force myself to get on the phone to someone who was working for a major search firm and offer him a job. I would tell them how great we were doing, how fast we were going to grow, that we were going to be *major,* man— and they thought I was out of my mind. This twenty-something kid in Cleveland who had never filled a job higher than middle management predicting that it was just a matter of time before his little company would be a major player in high-level searches in the technology business? To say I was met with incredulity is being kind to myself. Frankly, I didn't know when to shut up. I also had a sharp edge. Like a lot of entrepreneurs, I was arrogant; and only decades later did I realize that such arrogance is often a mask for fear. But at the time I just talked. I made the mistake of telling people all the things I knew were going to be true eventually. I hadn't yet learned that sometimes you can be too passionate for too long and lose your audience. Your enthusiasm can become counterproductive, and what you end up hearing at the other end of the phone is silence—or worse, laughter. In the face of such skepticism, I worked harder.

And then, in the late 1980s, the economy stumbled. Suddenly, we seemed less like a real company and more like a headquarters for a bunch of misfits specializing in making sure job applicants showed up on time for their interviews. My people had never bothered to cultivate long-term relationships either with their clients or with the top prospects in the job market. We had no network, no pipeline of talent. Earnings began to decrease. The company, which had been moving steadily uphill for years, was now tobogganing downward, straight toward the trees. To survive, I had to push off half of my employees.

The remnant hunkered down and rode out what proved to be a recession in the early 1990s. Then came the boom, which walked right into our arms. Technology companies were becoming the darlings of Wall Street, and we already had a reputation for being able to find high-tech managers. Suddenly we owned a big chunk of a very hot space, and I tried my damnedest to parlay it into contracts with bigger companies for higher-level searches. We created some clever marketing ploys; we hired people to specialize in researching candidates and companies, creating organizational breakdowns focusing on the jobs to be filled and the people in lower levels available for it. And to provide our staff with easy access to that research by computer, we even invested in information technology that established a growing database on all our searches: who was calling whom and when, the initial impressions of a candidate, the questions asked, responses from clients. Because we were based in Cleveland, the firm had to be quick with an answer to the question: How are you different? We were certainly way ahead of our competition in our use of information technology and research.

Yet the company did not budge. I had energy, I had enthusiasm, I did nothing else but work. The company was making money, but as an entrepreneur I was failing because I could not boost us up to the next level. Other search firms seemed to be growing faster while we were stalled in middle-management searches. I could not build the kind of credibility that persuaded clients that our firm was ready to recruit top managers, never mind CEOs. I learned that some businesses can survive for a while just by being there first. You can thrive on mere energy and perseverance—until, suddenly, you run into a wall.

It was a strange, confusing moment in my career. I knew I needed more talent around me, but my company did not have the visibility or the heat to attract it. And then I got lucky and hired two experienced headhunters, David Arnold and William (Kip) Schmidt. David had run his own search firm, working only on retainer. He was the first headhunter I met who had a genuine methodology for interviewing candidates. He knew how to probe into a manager's experience and personality to find out about their style of leadership, how they made things happen. My own interviewing style had been intuitive; David helped me add some technique to my natural instincts. Kip had worked for six years with

Russell Reynolds Associates, a major executive search firm with offices all around the country. He had a degree in electrical engineering and had worked eighteen years at Xerox in manufacturing, marketing, sales, and strategy, rising to a division vice president. When Russell Reynolds announced it was closing its Cleveland office, Kip decided that he didn't want to leave town. Instead, he took a chance on this new firm, where he used the network he had built up over the years in business and recruiting to bring in bigger accounts. He was also a great recruiter of recruiters.

We began analyzing the profiles of the kinds of people who succeeded in the firm, and of those who didn't. Some people could work fast and on deadline, we discovered, while others could not handle the heat. Some simply weren't interested in working hard enough. We also discovered that certain hires could be brilliant in their job interview—open, articulate, and with a personality that grabbed you by the lapels—but once they were in place, all that passion for communicating that so impressed us went into socializing around the office or on the phone and not headhunting. One thing was certain: our best people were also our smartest. We also learned that our best performers had already been successful in their previous jobs. Winners, even those from unrelated fields, tended to continue their winning streak as headhunters.

We made a decision right then: we had to be more intentional about our hiring; we had to create a bigger pipeline of talent, do more research on the people we were talking to; in short, we had to be as thorough when it came to hiring strategy for our own firm as we were for our clients. Through sheer luck some talented people had slipped into the company; we had to find more of the same. In fact, we had to hire the kind of people who were already so successful that they wouldn't ordinarily give Christian & Timbers a second thought. When we ran across extraordinarily talented prospects, we'd hire them even if we didn't need another employee and mark it down to investing in our future. As better companies started seeking us out, and we began working on more senior-level searches, I found myself talking to clients and candidates who were talented leaders. I began to notice patterns of leadership, personality traits that successful managers shared. I began to think harder about the meaning of talent and leadership. In the past, certain clients would claim that with brilliant managers on your side you could actually outperform a competitor who had a better product or technology. I would mark such statements down to hyperbole and go about my business trying to run my company. But then in the early 1990s, I worked with two companies in the same industry that needed new leadership to help them grow.

## THE DIFFERENCE IS TALENT

A decade ago, corporate executives were hitting the road all over America with their hard drives full of sales, marketing, and product-related data. These road warriors were eager for new ways to get this data from their computers and the Web onto projection screens. Two companies were positioned to take advantage of this growing multimedia market: InFocus, an Oregon projection-screen company with revenues of $60 million in 1992, and InFocus's major competitor, a small Virginia-based firm specializing in computer displays. By most accounts, InFocus's competitor had the right technology at the right time. In 1985, the company had developed a system to provide computer access to cerebral palsy victims by incorporating into overhead projectors the same kind of liquid crystal display (LCD) technologies used in laptop computers. After that success, the company developed award-winning LCD solutions for various commercial applications.

Today, this company is a publicly traded company doing quite nicely, producing flat panel displays used in industrial and corporate settings, from boardrooms and courtrooms to military bases. Meanwhile, InFocus has grown into a billion-dollar company, the world's biggest maker of data and video projectors, competing successfully against such better-known international giants as Sony, Hitachi, Epson, Sharp, and Philips. The difference, in my opinion, was one man—John Harker, a former consultant for Booz-Allen, whom InFocus hired as CEO in 1992. It was my first successful CEO search, and I don't think I had ever met anyone like John Harker. He exuded the kind of self-confidence you might expect in an ex-Navy pilot who was trained to fly an F-8 at twice the speed of sound and land it on an aircraft carrier that looks like a skillet bobbing in the ocean. "The reason you stay alive as an American aviator," Harker likes to say, "is that out there, a thousand feet up and off to your side, is a wingman." Over at InFocus's competitor, the founder-chairman was unwilling to bring in the kind of leadership that we believed that company needed to grow. He was not ready to figure out how to divide responsibilities for running the company; he was certainly not prepared to step aside; and he showed no propensity to anteing up the kind of compensation required to bring in a first-class CEO—like John Harker.

Harker, who went to work at IBM after leaving the Navy, has applied his respect for talent and love of competition to the multimedia business—"Second place is dead in a dogfight" is another favorite Harkerism. Talented people love working for him, and the company's technological breakthroughs prove it. In the decade since Harker took over, InFocus has introduced the first projector to combine data and video projection in a single box, the first sub-seven-pound personal projector, the first sub-five-pound projector, and the first "network" projector whose controls and content can be manipulated over the Worldwide Web.

Although Harker was my first CEO placement, even then I knew how lucky I was to find such an outstanding candidate. Another decade's experience recruiting top executives has only confirmed my luck: Harker remains at the top of my list of the most impressive business leaders I've ever met, and an indisputable example of what a difference talent can make for any company. I was determined to find more talent for my own company. In the course of that quest, I learned the value of developing an armor-plated ego, not to mention the ability to hear "no" over and over without getting discouraged. In fact, the people I wanted to hire most—for my company and for my clients—were the ones who did not want a job.

## THE MAIN TALENT FOR HIRING TALENT: PERSISTENCE

I have found that at least half of the good things in my career have happened late in the day, when I couldn't justify spending any more time at the office and then sat back down at my desk and made a few more phone calls. In 1994, I decided we needed an East Coast office, and I started looking for someone in the Boston area. One name kept coming up: Steve Mader, then working for J. Robert Scott, the executive search division of Fidelity Investments. I decided to give him a call. He turned me down flat. But I knew he was the right person to head our Boston office: he knew the business, he cared about quality, and he was a proven leader with eighteen years in operations. As VP of sales and marketing at Modicon, an industrial controls company, he had directed 500 employees worldwide and established a manufacturing and marketing joint venture in China. Above all, he would bring maturity and credibility to our young company.

I kept talking to him—and he turned me down two more times. I can remember sitting at home, talking on the phone with him for hours at a time, trying to persuade him to head our Boston office. He insisted he was happy in his current position; in fact, he was in the midst of making changes he wanted to finish. Impressed by how loyal he was to his company, I doubled my efforts to get him to transfer that kind of loyalty to Christian & Timbers. He finally accepted—and then backed out. I had to turn him around three times. I used every trick I knew to keep him talking, and never did I feel I was wasting my time, because I knew without any doubt that a strong professional like Steve Mader would make a huge difference to the future of my company. And I was right. Steve finally signed on, and soon those walls I kept crashing into disappeared. The bigger clients came, and so did the higher-level searches. Steve also accelerated our own efforts to recruit talented headhunters, and as our current president and COO, he's a constant contributor to the firm's recent success and growth.

I have yet to see the downside of persistence, though looking back at my escapades, some of the people at the other end of the phone must have wondered if they weren't dealing with a madman. In the late 1980s, Apple hired me to find a new VP of software. It was a giant step forward for our company, and I was thrilled. I was also scared. I set out to be as thorough as possible; if I didn't succeed, it would not be for lack of effort. I had heard about a great candidate, Nancy Shoendorf, a computer engineering graduate who had begun her career at HP and risen to director of systems software development at Sun Microsystems. She had reportedly taken some time off to raise a family. I made a few calls, got her home number in the Silicon Valley, and made the call. Her husband answered. Nancy was not at home, but I realized that I had actually worked on a search with Joe Shoendorf a few years before. That concerned me, because the search had not worked out. But Joe seemed friendly enough. I told him about the job I thought Nancy would be perfect for; he told me to give her a call. He also informed me that he was now with a venture-capital firm that was also looking for a VP of engineering for a new software company it was backing. I was planning a visit to Apple headquarters in nearby Cupertino, and we made a date to get together on a Friday, two days before Christmas. When I called him from my hotel on Thursday to firm up the time and place, Joe informed me that he had spoken to the software company's board about me but they preferred to work with a search firm with an office in the Silicon Valley. Once I caught my breath from this blow to the gut—I had spent several days preparing my presentation—I shifted into my scrambling mode. I assured him I was in the Silicon Valley so often that the staff at the Marriott saw me more than my own family. "We should talk," I said. He repeated that the company wanted to work with a local headhunter. "Give me a couple of hours," I said.

Two hours later I called him back. "I now have a California office." Shoendorf laughed, but I was serious. I had found one of those companies that rents office space and secretarial help to transient executives. I rented an office, and they gave me a business card with my new Silicon Valley address and phone number. Joe told me to come over to his house. I rushed to a nearby mall, and amid the throngs of last-minute Christmas shoppers and people singing Christmas carols, I bought a couple of quick presents for my host (a big chocolate-covered apple and a bottle of Dom Pérignon to wash it down) and then drove to his house in the hills, where Joe kindly listened to my presentation. Afterward, we had a good chat, but he once again raised the issue that I wasn't based in the Valley. "But I am," I said, and pulled out my new business card. Joe laughed again. "Give me a week or so. I'll see what I can do." This was a very nice man.

A week later, I called Joe, and he informed me that the company was adamant: They wanted to work with a headhunter who *lived* in the area. "If you give me a little time I can work that out, too," I said. He didn't think that would really change the board's mind. I suddenly felt as if I had overplayed my hand, and surely Joe now thought I was a jerk, or desperate for work, or both. But Joe actually apologized for not making it happen. "I'll tell you what," he said. "There's someone I want you to meet, a friend of mine. He has an important job, and he will need a lot of help." Joe assured me he would tell his friend to give me a call. A week later, Joe's friend called. His name was Lew Platt, then a Hewlett-Packard executive VP running half of HP's business. I had badgered Joe into spending the day before Christmas Eve with me as I pitched my company to him. For his trouble, I gave him a chocolate-covered apple. He helped me turn my company into the fastest-growing search firm in the nation. It was a great Christmas gift.

Lew Platt was absolutely committed to the Talent Principle. He gave me plenty of his time, and I tried to come up with great candidates. The first big search I did for HP was to recruit Gary Eichorn from Digital Equipment to run HP's workstation business. A rising star at DEC and on every recruiter's short list of potential CEOs, Eichorn was a good get for HP. For my company, it was a triumph. We did fifteen more searches for Hewlett-Packard.

Then one morning in the spring of 1999, I picked up the paper and saw a story reporting that Platt had decided to retire. That story and others I read predicted that HP would be looking to either Gerard Roche, a top recruiter at Heidrick & Struggles, or another heavy hitter, Tom Neff, at Spencer Stuart, to do the search for Platt's successor. I tended to agree, because when companies with reputations like HP set out to fill the CEO slot, they typically turned to the HPs of the search business. I also began rationalizing why HP was right to ignore small companies like mine and go with the big guys: I had never done such a high-level search for such a major company; Platt, my main ally at the company, was the person they were replacing; and he wasn't on the search committee. To forgo the pain of rejection, I decided not to even bother calling HP about the assignment.

And then I picked up the phone and called Lew Platt, who generously recommended me to the search committee, which, contrary to reports in the press, had not made a decision on the search firm; they invited me to make a presentation to the head of the committee. I did not just give this project my best shot—I went with both barrels and then grabbed a side gun. I already knew the company well, which allowed me to spend all my time researching a preliminary list of potential candidates, including a few I thought ought to be at the top of their list. Three of my names were people

I had been in contact with about other searches, including someone who was at the top of HP's list. The committee awarded me
first try at filling the job. The deal was that I had to produce results
within thirty days. If I did not deliver in that time frame, they
would hire one of the old-guard search firms.

With the help of my colleagues and some CEOs at major corporations in our network, I made sure I was not leaving anyone out.
We started with a hundred names and then targeted twenty-five.
The pool of executives that is clearly capable of running a $40 bil-
lion company is never large, but among the best candidates, HP
sparked a lot of interest. We narrowed the field down to a list of
six finalists, which we presented to the search committee. With
their help and some further scrutiny, we cut the slate down to four.
My favorite was someone I had put on our initial target list and
hardly anybody's obvious choice early on in the search process—
Carleton S. Fiorina, the forty-four-year-old president of Lucent
Technologies' $20 billion Global Service Provider Business, the
company's largest and fastest-growing division. Fiorina had done
such a brilliant job organizing Lucent's spin-off from AT&T in
1996 that *Fortune* had named her the most powerful woman in
American business.

Unfortunately, I had never met Carly Fiorina. And every time I
called her office, the secretary stonewalled me. After four calls, I
was ready to give up. Then late in the workday I tried her number
at Lucent one last time. Fiorina herself picked up the phone. I explained why I was calling, and she agreed to meet with me to discuss the HP job. I flew to New Jersey, and 107 days later Carly
Fiorina was the new CEO of Hewlett-Packard. The announcement
that Fiorina would succeed Lew Platt—and thus become the first
female to lead either a Dow 30 or Fortune 50 company—grabbed

front-page headlines all over America. A few of the stories were kind enough to mention that the search firm of Christian & Timbers had played matchmaker.

When talent is in the balance, you can never make too many phone calls.

## TALENT IS ALWAYS THE SOLUTION

Businesses run into a lot of walls. Mine certainly did, and what I learned from so many crashes is that the only way to recover is with talented people. You cannot boost your business to the next step unless you take time out from the day-to-day problems of running a business to upgrade your associates. That will not happen if you let talented job candidates sit in the reception area wondering why they have come all this way to read last month's copy of *Fortune*. Thriving in a Talent Economy is not about just filling jobs; *it is putting people on your balance sheet as your highest valued asset.* The best people you can find for every job. The most talented people. And, as I finally learned, you will have to keep calling them, romance them, persuade them that their best future is with you. You will even have to get on a plane and chase after them. A few years ago, we found a terrific candidate for a big job, and our client agreed. He made her an offer, and she headed off for a week's vacation in Hawaii to think it over. That was a problem. She was such a find that we knew she would be sitting on the beach thinking over several other offers along with ours. So we told our client, "Fly to Hawaii, meet with her, take her to dinner—and don't allow her a minute to contemplate those other job offers." That CEO flew to Hawaii, spent as much time with her as possible, and she ended up taking the job. That is what exceptional business leaders do. In fact, this almost fanatical commitment to talent is, in my opinion, what makes some leaders exceptional. What is my definition of "talent"? It is probably different from yours. Most people in business are looking for experience. A headhunter is more likely to focus on certain personality traits. But the first thing you have to understand is how talent is related to leadership—and how leaders cannot succeed without people who are more talented than they are.

## CHAPTER 2

# The Formula for Exceptional Leadership

Even after I started focusing on hiring better people, a prime obstacle to growing my company persisted: me. As the founder and CEO, I was clearly the firm's leader. The trouble was, my leadership style was more appropriate to running the Soviet Union than leading an executive recruiting firm eager to take on high-level management and CEO searches. My idea of leading was to have all the ideas and make all the decisions. I was willing to listen to other people's ideas, but I was inclined to believe mine were better. That kind of arrogance eventually sent my original colleague for the exit, and it was hardly the kind of attitude that would make me a beacon for talent. What strong player at a major search firm would want to hook up with an unpredictable twenty-something entrepreneur who wanted to get his way all the time?

As I began to work on higher-level searches, I made a conscious effort to learn what my best clients and candidates knew about leadership. I would grill the CEOs and high-level managers I was working with about how much time they spent on hiring and what qualities they looked for in people. They became my business school. I asked them how they created businesses and grew them. I asked them how they made big changes, fired people, created new business strategies and abandoned old ones. I interrogated turn-around specialists on the details of reorganizing a troubled company. Above all, I tried to find out how they led their people toward profits and growth. It was then that I began to understand the intimate connection between leadership and talent. The best leaders I met struck me as being truly a breed apart—smart, driven, passionate, the kind of people others will follow into machine-gun fire. They did not seem to need any help. Soon I discovered, however, that what separated exceptional leaders from the rest was that they were the first to admit how much help they needed.

Leadership is a powerful weapon in business, which is why every company wants it. Leadership is one of those things that we all think we know, until someone asks us to spell it out. How does a short Italian-born soldier emerge as France's incomparable Napoleon? What was it about an unattractive country lawyer that made him Lincoln? How did a gentleman's C student at Harvard who spent a large portion of his adult life confined to a wheelchair with polio emerge as FDR? Business executives have their icons, too. But one also wonders what there was in Jack Welch that took a lifelong stutterer and turned him into a CEO's CEO, or how an antisocial college dropout named Bill Gates created the first monopoly of the computer world? And how did a medieval history and philosophy major like Carly Fiorina earn the title as the most powerful female executive in America *before* she was named CEO of Hewlett-Packard?

To be sure, many of the most successful managers in business were born leaders. But I know from personal experience that there is plenty you can learn. I advise young people that they will increase their odds for getting the job of their dreams if they polish their leadership skills and work on their defects in college or business school. Young managers should do the same on the job. The rest of us must keep trying to become better leaders. In 1992, I finally vowed to do that. I had to start listening to the talent that I had brought into my company. They did not disagree. To improve the leadership in our company, we began by creating a more democratic management system. We set up a "Business Committee," each member wielding a single vote. It was a perfect way to curtail my own dictatorial urges and prove the benefits of sharing power and listening to the smart people I'd hired. Even though I remain the largest shareholder in the firm, I have conceded my right to overrule my colleagues. Whenever I'm tempted to insist on having my own way—and I will confess that it happens to me many times—all I have to do is remind myself of the days when I couldn't recruit people who were anywhere near as strong as my current partners.

## WHAT LEADERSHIP IS NOT

No subject has been more written about in business and less understood than "leadership." There are thousands of titles in print; at any given time, any large bookstore will have a hundred or so books on "leadership" and "management" and "strategic thinking" on its shelves. Psychologists and academics have published forests of treatises on the attitudes and behaviors that distinguish top executives from the also-rans. The subject is a staple of corporate training and business school classes. So why listen to me? For starters, my colleagues and I are familiar with a lot of the literature on leadership, and most of it will either make your eyes glaze over or is obvious or superficial. In my twenty years as a headhunter, I have been interviewing two hundred top managers and CEOs a year, and somewhere in the middle of those four thousand or so interviews, I began to see patterns in their personalities and management styles. I also realized that genuine leadership in business is not what most businessmen (or business journalists) think it is. Yes, you have to have the personal desire to excel, but having it will not necessarily make you an excellent leader. Hard work is crucial, but taking your sleeping bag to the office will not turn you into Jack Welch or Carly Fiorina. Neither will a well-cut suit, a gift for gab, a trim body, or a scratch golf game. A glittering résumé will not make you a leader. Just look around you and see how many top graduates of the Harvard Business School, or Stanford, or Wharton, are warming the benches in middle management, while C-minus students and college dropouts are revolutionizing the global marketplace. Everyone has read that two of the founding fathers of the personal computer revolution, Steve Jobs and Bill Gates, dropped out of college, but did you know that Gordon Bethune, the CEO who in the 1990s saved Continental Airlines from a near-death experience, left high school and joined the Navy?

Leadership is not even about experience. No U.S. president gets to practice running a smaller country, and, similarly, most great CEOs are first-time chief executives. Lee Iacocca rose through the ranks at Ford, as did Jack Welch at General Electric; Cisco's John Chambers was elevated to chief executive from senior VP of World Wide Sales after fourteen years at Wang and IBM; Herb Kelleher was practicing law when a client came to him with an idea for a cut-rate airline that became Southwest. Lew Gerstner spent eleven years as a top executive at American Express before getting the top job at RJR Nabisco, and then four years later at IBM. Every candidate short-listed for any top job is likely to have the basic management skills and experience required. It is definitely not technical knowledge that will turn you into a legendary leader. In fact, CEOs hired only for their experience usually get fired for lack of integrity, laziness, and the kind of poor leadership that fills organizations with chaos or resentment rather than innovation—reasons that have nothing to do with knowledge or experience. Nor do venture capitalists or corporate analysts expect management perfection in top executives. When evaluating great leaders, they often go by the principle "Mistakes are expected; failure is not."

## WHAT IS EXCEPTIONAL LEADERSHIP?

Frankly, I find it harder to define leadership than to sense it. Like all holy grails, leadership is a mysterious thing. When friends and young hires at Christian & Timbers ask me how I know a person is (or has the potential to be) an exceptional business leader, my first inclination is to say, "I know it when I see it." Recently, I interviewed a candidate as a CEO prospect for a major telecommunications company. I was interested in him because he was already running the international operations of one of the best networking companies in the world, reporting directly to the CEO. It was already clear to him that he was not the heir apparent (the competition, he explained, had an edge on him in experience), but like just about every talented person I've ever met, he wanted to run his own show. I was then in the process of filling two CEO positions, and he was particularly interested in one of them. We met, and I was underwhelmed. I checked him out further, and the references were good. He was well respected in the industry. I still didn't think he had the leadership ability for the job. But on the strength of his résumé and references, plus the client's curiosity to meet him, the company brought him in for an interview. My client ended up as unimpressed as I had been. The guy just did not exude leadership.

What was he missing, precisely? For many of my clients, their notion of a good leader tends to be what they can most easily see: impressive credentials, experience, reputation, poise, grooming, charm, swagger, the ability to manage their own and others' emotions, or management style. And while it is true that certain great leaders exude an unmistakable aura—from childhood we've all known the kind of person everyone else just follows—I have also met managers who have a less charismatic style but whose leadership nevertheless produces exceptional results. As a headhunter, I do not want to miss out on a quiet but exceptional leader. In fact, most professional recruiters recognize that most of the qualities that make someone a leader aren't as obvious as a résumé that reveals a trajectory of jobs rising ever upward. Leadership is defined by certain personality characteristics—what we call "soft skills" or "innate traits"—that are related to an executive's attitude toward work, his confidence, how he talks, the questions he asks, the ease with which he operates, the kinds of people he hires, and how he treats them. In an interview, I know I am talking to a potential leader if they are impatient and do not have the time to talk to me; and when they do meet with me, they are eager to take control of the conversation; they speak clearly and concisely, getting quickly to the tough questions, often ones you had not anticipated. Good leaders are master strategists; they are always well prepared; and when you're in the same room with them, you can almost see that strategic sense controlling the meeting. Leadership has a lot to do with how someone exhibits himself in a very short time. In my experience, exceptional leaders have a quiet intensity about them; you feel you can trust them. Almost immediately, you can feel their depth and strength, and you want to follow them.

This particular candidate had an enviable résumé; he even looked like a leader. But to me and my client, he fell short in the intangibles. For starters, he didn't seem prepared for my interview. I would ask one of my standard questions—"Tell me about something you tried that didn't turn out so well, and what you learned from it"—and he would say, "What an unusual question!" and then think about it for a while. In fact, it was not such an unusual question, and I was certainly not looking for any kind of paradigm-busting answer that might require the amount of thought he gave it. Ten minutes into the interview, I began wondering whether there weren't more reasons why he was not first in line to succeed the CEO at his current company other than experience.

It is at moments like this, when leadership is not present in the room, that I flash on the best leaders I have interviewed. Once you have come in contact with the genuine article, it is hard to settle for second best.

## HARD EVIDENCE FOR SOFT SKILLS: TWO OF THE MOST IMPRESSIVE LEADERS I'VE MET

I got my first jolt of exceptional leadership when I interviewed John Harker for the InFocus CEO search. I was looking for a leader, but it wasn't until I met Harker that I really knew what leadership was. He was interviewing for a big job, but I was the nervous one. I'm sure John sensed the tension on my side, and he quickly put me at ease with his relaxed style and humor. His intelligence and passion were immediately evident, and that self-confidence of the Navy fighter pilot was something that any headhunter would want a client to experience. When he talked about his work, you sensed how close to every aspect he was; you could see his thought patterns taking shape. You felt that this was an executive for whom success was routine. Harker had a reputation for making everyone feel good about what they were doing. Honest and intense, he treated people with respect and he made complex missions so clear and simple that everyone understood their roles. Talented managers flocked to Harker, and within eight years his new team transformed InFocus from a scrappy young company with revenues of $60 million into a giant killer with revenues of almost $400 million. In 2000, Harker merged InFocus with its main rival, Proxima, a Norwegian company, boosting sales to $900 million in 2001.

John Harker also has another quality that I had trouble putting my finger on at the time because I was so green about exceptional leadership. Quite a few years and thousands of interviews later, I realize that his mysterious something is common among exceptional leaders—a quiet self-assurance, the ability to project the kind of credibility and trust that makes employees break through walls to win their approval. I've also learned that such muted confidence is not necessarily a guy thing. I also saw it in Carly Fiorina.

Once we met in person, I knew she was the real deal. Fiorina is very smart, but so are a lot of executives. She is intense, but that, too, is a given in most of the top people I interview. I was also impressed by the confidence she had about herself and her work. But what really grabbed me about Carly Fiorina was her humility. It's not a quality most people usually identify with CEOs, but it is amazing how many of the best top executives I've met have a more realistic sense of their own skills than the PR department. In twenty years of interviewing executives, I have found that the ability to recognize your limitations is one of the crucial soft skills for leadership. Fiorina, for example, was very quick to inform me that she was "no technologist." That was not her strength; but she had spent her career surrounding herself with talented technicians she could trust. Nor did she claim to have every answer. When someone else deserved credit, she gave it. You got the sense from her that she had her own methodology for getting things done. As she described her work at Lucent, she was able to take me into a very deep level of detail: how she shifted organizations around, rebuilt them, restructured them. She was able to relate to me the actual thought processes she went through as she planned and executed these changes. There was no doubt in my mind that she had done precisely what she said. When she discussed her customers, it was clear to me she knew them well, listened to them, cared about them. She was *passionate* about her connection to customers. Exceptional leaders deal with all their constituencies well—the board, their management team, employees, and customers—another skill that is invisible on résumés. In Carly's case it was that intimate understanding of the people she was selling to that allowed her to anticipate their technology needs two to three years down the road. By listening to her customers, she was able to place the right bets and beat the competition to the next great technology.

Once Fiorina signed on at HP, her intelligence and energy were never in doubt. She got amazing publicity. A woman running such a company was a big story, and Carly's efforts to rebrand HP made her an even better story. She initiated a huge ad campaign aimed at informing the public that HP, a famous Old Economy electronics company founded in a Palo Alto garage in 1938 by two Stanford students with $538 to play with, not only had distinguished itself in the Computer Age but was already an innovator at the center of the Internet Era. Fiorina also focused on talent immediately, taking time to meet with all her managers at breakfasts and in small discussion groups, engaging them in her vision of the future. Even people inside HP who lost out to her for the CEO job stayed on, in spite of calls from headhunters offering them the top jobs at other firms. She also brought in some top managers from the outside. Inside the company, her intelligence, drive, and leadership style were immediately infectious. Of course, not everyone bought her vision. Agents of change will always stir up critics. She jettisoned some HP traditions, instituting, for example, incentive packages that fired up her sales force. In any established company with a deep culture like HP, many people will prefer the way it was, and some engineers have left. She also made some risky bets, and her critics were watching the results very carefully. But she had been hired to drive sales and increase profits, and she proceeded to do that during her first year.

Fiorina handled the hoopla over her ascent with great charm and patience. But what impressed me even more about her as a leader was how she handled the criticism when the receding economy of 2001 left HP, and most other computer-related firms, with increased inventories and decreased profits. Wall Street was particularly frosty, and HP stock fell lower than it had been in a year. The same publications that had heralded her arrival at HP hammered her for being too optimistic about earnings. Others pointed fingers at Fiorina for her role in Lucent's slide in 2000. Fiorina stayed as cool about the criticism from the business press as she was about their earlier praise. Even with her stock in the cellar and when most CEOs would be scrambling for short-term fixes, Fiorina announced a massive program to sell products in the Third World. "Smart people are not confined to the developed world," she explained. Fiorina's plan is for HP and its partners to sell, lease, or donate a billion dollars' worth of products and services to Third World governments, development agencies, and nonprofits. The early focus of what Fiorina calls her "e-Inclusion" program will be increasing the efficiency of small farmers who make up half of the income of countries like Senegal and Bangladesh. HP will also work closely with micro-credit experts to find better ways of financing Third World entrepreneurs eager to grow their small manufacturing companies or get more innovative—for instance, by introducing cell-phone service in remote areas where phone service is either very expensive or not available at all. A *Fortune* columnist called Fiorina's plan to do well by doing good "the most visionary step I've ever seen a large tech company take."

In the fall of 2001, Fiorina enlarged the HP vision in an even bigger way, jolting the troubled computer industry with the announcement that HP would spend $23 billion to acquire one of its biggest competitors, Compaq Computer. Critics of the merger were quick to wonder about the advantage of merging companies already too focused on the production of PCs, hardly the new thing in technology. But the combined company would rival IBM in size and revenue, and could conceivably speed by Dell in PC sales. Whatever the pluses and minuses of the HP-Compaq merger, Fiorina had proven once again that she was not afraid to make a big, risky decision—even one that threatened her job. Exceptional business leaders move ahead with their vision even if they have to wait for the economy—and their critics—to catch up. Carly remained her audacious self, pointing to the undeniable fact that HP had exceeded Wall Street expectations in the final quarter of 2001 and the first quarter of 2002. As I write, sons of both cofounders of Hewlett-Packard are stirring up opposition to the Compaq merger among HP shareholders, even though the company's board has backed the deal. The irony of this conflict has not been lost on Fiorina's fellow CEOs around the country. Headhunters, too, cannot resist raising an eyebrow. I have spent my career replacing founders of struggling companies with professional leaders. Who would have thought that a company as big and sophisticated as Hewlett-Packard would be fending off founders' sons—who do not work for the company—for control of the overall corporate vision? In my experience, a company can have only one leader. Carly Fiorina has not shied away from the fight. If she wins, her next challenge will be to create one culture in the new, combined company. And if that weren't tough enough, Fiorina will also have to lower costs and prove to employees, customers, and shareholders that her new vision for HP is a profitable one—all under the intense scrutiny of the media. Has there ever been a CEO of such a large company with so many distractions? As the first woman to run a Fortune 20 company, Fiorina has always worked in the glare of a constant spotlight, but now she also gets to hear the sound of a ticking clock. While she mounted an all-out defense of the HP-Compaq merger, the competition was working just as hard to grab market share from two companies with a question mark over their futures. It used to be that the markets gave a major brand in turnaround a long honeymoon (it took Lew Gerstner seven years to work his magic on IBM); in today's speeded up and struggling economy, Fiorina may have no more than another eighteen months to generate some impressive numbers. If she fails to deliver, no one can take away her title as the first woman to run a Fortune 20 company (or her number one ranking for four years in a row on Fortune's list of "The Most Powerful Women" in American business). And if Carly decides to leave HP, my bet is that she will get another opportunity to run another big company. Leaders with her talent—and experience under fire—are not likely to be allowed to sit on the sidelines.

## CAN LEADERSHIP BE LEARNED?

Fair question. I cannot teach you to be extremely intelligent or to turn your memory into a hard drive of instantly retrievable information, data, and strategy. Nor can you buy extraordinary physical energy (at least not legally). Nevertheless, there are many things that the great natural-born leaders do that you can learn. Over the years, I have found that there are several common qualities or personality traits that exceptional leaders share. Everyone in the executive search business has a personal list of what to look for in an executive. I have a shortlist of five qualities that I think define "leadership" today.

## THE "FORMULA FIVE" OF
## EXCEPTIONAL LEADERSHIP

1. **Honesty and Integrity** Exceptional leaders are able to build a deep level of trust in organizations in a flash—an absolute requirement for turning around a company in trouble. Major change is always hard for an organization to take, and without an environment of trust, change will only be resented. Leaders must ask their employees to take risks, to work under the burden of uncertainty, and make some sacrifices to ensure a better future for everyone in the company. To take a step into an abyss, people must believe that the leader is operating in their best interests and not only in his own. To borrow some wisdom about leadership from the New Testament (1 Corinthians 14:8): "If the trumpet give an uncertain sound, who shall prepare himself to the battle?" Engendering trust requires a mission and principles that everyone understands. Great leaders are principled people, and, fortunately, that is a quality that is hard to fake. Integrity entails honesty, and that means being honest about yourself. Most people who have worked for a faker or a blowhard will appreciate a boss who can be critical of himself, who knows his weaknesses as well as his strengths. Principled leaders tend to be strong, but with no pretense of infallibility. They surround themselves with top executives who can complement them, and they trust them. Honesty and integrity are qualities that you sense in a person. You just feel good around them. After decades of interviewing executives, I have learned that in cases where everything seems fine about a candidate, and the person seems to match the résumé, and the references check out . . . yet something *still*

seems a bit off, there is usually an integrity problem. These candidates end up being a little bit more crooked than they seemed. Companies that are not careful recruiters often get pressured into making a decision on a candidate even though something is bothering them. A candidate of genuine honesty and integrity will not leave you feeling a little queasy.

**2. Intellectual Firepower** Great business leaders are smart. Scary smart. They have phenomenal memories and are a storehouse of information and data. They can distill a complex situation down to the basic components for action; they can juggle multiple ideas and tasks simultaneously—and successfully. In new situations they vacuum up the most crucial information and can see problems from different perspectives. They have an eerie ability to ask the one essential question you have not anticipated. They are also smart enough to admit when they do not have the answer. Exceptional leaders have gotten where they are not just because they are flat-out smart, but because they always know that they have more to learn.

**3. Energy and Passion** Most CEOs could retire and head south to work on their golf games, but great leaders are not in it only for the money. They love what they do. They also know that at their level, what they do affects the lives and fortunes of thousands of employees, not to mention millions of customers and fellow citizens. The success of major companies affects the economic future of us all. Exceptional leaders get up in the morning and head to the office with a bounce in their step, knowing that what they do can make a difference. They also have a sense that they're lucky, which is why they love putting themselves on the line to make things happen. That kind of passion, energy, and drive is contagious. Exceptional leaders tend to have the stamina of trained athletes, and this kind of tireless work ethic inspires their corporate teams, driving them to success. When there seems to be nowhere else to go, they find a new direction. But leadership is more than a brute stamina that keeps you going 24/7. The energy of great leaders is focused; they know exactly what they are doing, where they are going, and they can articulate these goals. Great leaders actually like solving problems and being challenged. They know that problem solvers rise to the top and that the definition of a career is a series of new and increasing challenges. They also know that they will not win every battle. There will be setbacks. But what separates great leaders from the also-rans is that they can take on situations where everyone else has failed and succeed. Above all, their energy and drive are a magnet for other talent, inside and outside the company. Talent is drawn to talent. Who doesn't want to be part of a major success story?

4. Leadership You can have all of the above qualities and still not be a leader. One of the great revelations I made early in my own career in business was that the people with the most impressive credentials (the silver-spoon upbringing, the Ivy League degrees, the top B-schools, even the class A starter jobs at McKinsey or Booz-Allen) do not always have the most successful careers in the corporate world. How satisfying to discover that what makes you teacher's pet might also turn you into lunch in the marketplace. A Phi Beta Kappa Key will make your mother proud, but the person who is most likely to rise is the manager who's smart enough to know that he doesn't know everything and surrounds himself with

talent. In my experience, what separates leaders from intelligent, enthusiastic workaholics is strong decision-making skills and the ability to take a group of diverse people with even more diverse talents and abilities and transform them into a unique corporate culture. Just as Napoleon or de Gaulle *became* France, or Churchill *became* Great Britain during World War II, great CEOs set the tone and style of their domains. They distill a vision of where the organization should be going. Genuine leaders recognize that playing the dictator is counterproductive. They know that they can acquire more power by inspiring their people to help with the mission and grow the enterprise. Eager to make people feel they're doing something important, they are quick to deal praise. When leaders approach a turnaround situation, they find out from their managers—and customers—what their predecessor was not doing right. Above all, leaders get the right talent into the right jobs, and the wrong people out of the organization.

5. Humility Exceptional leaders know what they do not know and are not afraid to admit it. In interviews I like to ask top managers this question: "What did you do a couple of years ago that today you wished you had done better?" The best leaders have a *lot* of examples. Humble people, I have found, are people who are always learning, and good leaders must be learning all the time. It is this kind of self-knowledge and humility that drives them to hire the best people to fill in their gaps. Because such leaders understand that they are not infallible, and they allow their people to make mistakes and learn from them. Humility encourages managers to create a learning environment—a primary variable for success in today's Talent Economy.

This "Formula Five" offers a high standard of leadership. For me, it is Everest. But the list can also be a useful measure for your own standing as a leader. Be honest about how you stack up, and then get to work. I repeat: *leadership is something you can learn.* And the most crucial thing to learn is that you cannot learn to be a leader without surrounding yourself with the best talent you can find.

Do great leaders have to be nice guys? No. But transmitting your passion and getting your managers committed to the mission will not be easy if the troops have been terrorized. Find a middle ground where innovation and accountability can coexist. Leaders inspire the people under them. They know when a pat on the back—or a boot in the butt—will get people to do a better job. Although they might not be "fun people," good leaders are fun to work for because they create environments where people are winning and making things happen, where everyone feels connected to the larger vision. We all know that when we're allowed to do what we are best at, when a work environment encourages innovation, going to the office every day is a joy. That does not necessarily mean that the office is one big, wild party. But genuine leaders create successful companies, and there is nothing more fun in business than being successful. To find that middle ground between Captain Kangaroo and Captain Queeg, you can also *untrain* yourself from all sorts of bad habits. Above all:

- Don't be a control freak. It is not easy to loosen up on the reins, especially for entrepreneurs who are used to doing it their way (or who, in many instances, invented the way to do it). The key is: instead of telling people what they ought to do, ask them what they think they should do. I promise you will be amazed by how often you arrive in the same place.

- Don't be autocratic, even when it comes to setting the strategy to achieve your mission. Skilled leaders understand that the best way to get people committed to a strategy is to let them think they thought it up. "Here's where we need to go; here's the problem we have getting there. How would you solve it?" If you've hired talented people, they will have answers. Even when they're sure they have the answer, smart leaders are hoping that someone might come up with a better way. The best leaders hire great performers and let them perform. As I learned in my own business, talent does not enjoy working for someone who has all the answers.

- Don't be a bully. One's first and very natural reaction in the face of an obvious mistake is to get angry and impatient: "Okay, you screwed up, it's your fault, now fix it!" That is not leadership. It's petulance or bullying. To be sure, the angry response can get results; but in the long run, such behavior creates fear and loathing, not loyalty.

- Don't overmeasure or undermeasure. Exceptional leaders know exactly the right things to measure. We have overprocessed and underprocessed in my own company, so count me a learner in this regard. There were times when we were measuring only revenue and profits, forgetting things that are crucial to success such as employee retention and satisfaction. Smart leaders are also eager to satisfy their customers, and that requires listening to them and delivering on the basis of what they say.

- Don't underestimate the talent you already have. It is amazing to me how many companies do not even bother to evaluate the quality and success of their own management teams. It could be that you already own some of the best talent in your business. But you have to know how good your people are, and then give them a chance to keep proving it.

One of the best ways to learn the finer points of leadership is to analyze the careers of top managers you admire, with particular attention to those who have been up against the same kind of challenges you are facing. The great careers in business tend to be defined by certain achievements. Some legends are known for creating companies, others for growing them. Some are turnaround specialists, who come in from the outside. In my own personal analysis, I quickly discovered that the main question the best CEOs and managers I talked to asked was: "Who's the talent around me?" The best performers I interviewed, executives who had already proven they could run a business, always asked about the people in the company. They also talked about bringing people in—and letting people go. Turnaround specialists discussed how they set up an organization; they, too, were concerned about the skills of the managers they would inherit and were eager to bring in some outside help. The best performers I talked to knew they could not do it alone. "Who's in the game?" and "Who can I bring with me?" were questions I heard all the time.

I began to understand that success in business depended on how committed managers were to surrounding themselves with a garden of talent—and then spending a great chunk of their time cultivating it. Consider two of America's greatest business leaders, General Electric's Jack Welch and IBM's Lew Gerstner. Both men have been written about often, but rarely from the point of view of how much of their focus—and success—is due to their passion for finding, nourishing, and rewarding talent.

## MAESTROS OF TALENT:
## MR. OUTSIDE AND MR. INSIDE

In the early nineties, IBM was deep in the doldrums as smaller computer companies began to gobble up what Big Blue's executives viewed to be the company's birthright. IBM's slide was proof that "blue chip" was not forever. (Recently, Coca-Cola and Procter & Gamble have provided additional evidence.) In 1992, IBM reported its worst annual loss—$8.70 a share. The following year, the IBM board brought in Gerstner, who had been chairman and CEO of RJR Nabisco for four years and for eleven years before that had been a top executive at American Express. Gerstner's customer-oriented sensibility combined with a knack for strategic thinking (honed early in his career as a management consultant at McKinsey) was exactly what the IBM board thought the company needed.

Gerstner was also the first IBM chief to come from the outside. One look at IBM and the new CEO reportedly recognized that "the company was utterly dysfunctional, that nobody told their boss the truth." Considering that IBM had about 400,000 employees worldwide at the time, a widespread lack of candor promised to be a costly business problem. When one supplier tried to return $20,000 that IBM had mistakenly overpaid, the IBM manager he was dealing with refused the check—and thus evidence that the great IBM might actually have screwed up. Division managers were more concerned with perpetuating current staff and budget levels than they were with satisfying customers. The company had grown bloated and slow-witted. Even when its best brains came up with a new idea, management was slow at turning it into a product and getting it to market. "That was a much bigger institutional shortcoming than a lack of innovation," Gerstner recently conceded. To reverse the company's slide into the red, he began cutting costs and rebuilding the product line.

He also chopped off a lot of heads. As an experienced CEO who had also worked as a corporate consultant, Gerstner knew he would have a honeymoon period. The advantage of turning around a major brand like IBM is that the brand itself adds value to the company, even when it's in trouble. Wall Street and the press have a built-in respect for a major American brand like IBM. No one wants to see a sure Hall of Famer lose it. Gerstner quickly began looking for the problems and for ways to fix them. Despite pressure to split IBM up into separate, smaller companies, the new CEO stuck with his own vision: to take advantage of one of IBM's strong points—the ability of a large, multilayered company to provide integrated solutions to customers. He also branded himself as a strong and tough leader who promised to make IBM profitable and keep it growing. And he delivered. IBM is not only impressively profitable again, but the company was virtually the lone major tech to sail through the economic downturn making money and boosting its stock price. As I write, IBM's market capitalization stands at ten times the value Gerstner found it when he became CEO. His achievement is widely regarded as one of the most extraordinary turnarounds in U.S. corporate history.

At the core of Gerstner's strategy was talent. In mammoth, successful companies like IBM, too many top managers end up coasting on their reputations. But Gerstner was not an IBM lifer; he had no attachments to the past. He had no compunctions about getting rid of someone just because some VP said, "Well, I've known Bob for thirty years. I can't fire him." As the first leader at IBM from outside the company, he didn't give a damn about Bob; he didn't know Bob. All he knew was what he had to do to turn IBM's flab back into muscle. He fired all those Bobs, brought in a bunch of people who were as talented as Bob was thirty years ago and who were not overawed by the old IBM's white-shirt, dark-suit culture.

In 1995, Gerstner's IBM announced it would look for growth in its networking business—and began acquiring companies like Lotus Development and Tivoli Systems, to amass the talent and technology that would put IBM back into contention. IBM now owns seven microchip companies. Gerstner was even willing to acknowledge that IBM could not be all things to all customers and in that same year began making strategic alliances with producers of software applications for businesses. By January 2001, IBM had nearly 100,000 such alliances in place—a source of more than a third of the company's revenues by then. The press marveled at how "one man" had created a new IBM. Lew Gerstner, however, knew he'd had lots of help from his managers. But it was definitely one man—one leader—who knew that he had to find out who his best people were, hire more, and let them loose.

No American CEO has been better at hiring, managing, and keeping talent than GE's Jack Welch, whom *Fortune* has described as "the leading management revolutionary of the [twentieth] century" as well as "the most widely admired, studied, and imitated CEO of his time." One publisher paid $7.1 million for Welch to tell how he did it (a *little* bit more than what I'm getting to share my knowledge). What would-be imitators should focus on is the way Welch wages war for talent. During his twenty-year tenure as GE's chief executive, Welch has turned the company into the most impressive talent machine in business. Every other company wants to recruit one of Welch's lieutenants. Few dare. Welch has been known to get on the phone and inform the CEO who is poaching one of his managers that he is risking never doing business with GE again, no matter how profitable to GE their current relationship might be. As Welch approaches the end of his career, the media has made him into a genial elder statesman, ignoring what a bare-knuckled Irish brawler he has always been. After all, this is a boss who likes to call the company's top young managers "black belts."

Regarding those employees who do not measure up, Welch is most unsentimental. When he took over GE in 1980 and began massive layoffs, the press labeled him "Neutron Jack." Welch has his standards, and over the years he institutionalized them. GE uses what Welch calls the "four *E*'s" to pick its leaders: (1) *energy*—required to keep up with the "frenetic pace of change," Welch has said; (2) *energize*—the ability to inspire an organization to action; (3) *edge*—the self-confidence to make the tough calls, one way or the other; (4) *execute*—what Welch calls "the ancient GE tradition" of always delivering. The company also evaluates its leaders according to four "types." This is how Welch has described these different kinds of managers and their futures at General Electric:

Type I: shares our values; makes our numbers—sky's the limit!
Type II: doesn't share the values; doesn't make the numbers—gone. Type III: shares the values, misses the numbers—typically, another chance or two. Type IV: is the toughest call of all: the manager who doesn't share the values, but delivers the numbers; the "go-to" manager, the hammer, who delivers

the bacon but does it on the backs of people, often "kissing up and kicking down" during the process.

Type IV is a goner, too, and is strong evidence for how committed Welch is to the Talent Principle. Most leaders as bottom-line oriented as Welch would not be able to jettison a "go-to" guy who consistently makes his numbers. "But," explains Welch, "we have to remove these Type IV's because they have the power, by themselves, to destroy the open, informal, trust-based culture we need to win today and tomorrow." For Welch, trust is what makes a company innovative; managers are allowed to take chances, knowing that it's GE's policy that a "miss" doesn't equal "career damage." To make the point that the company is really committed to such "soft" values as integrity and trust, Welch fires Type IV's and makes it clear to the entire company that they were asked to go not "for personal reasons" or "to pursue other opportunities," but simply because they had rejected GE's values.

GE is famous for finding great leaders among its own employees and moving them up through the ranks, testing the most successful performers with one challenge after another. Welch knows who his A players are because he devotes a big chunk of his time to checking the results of the company's evaluation and reward systems. He has divided GE's 300,000 employees into three categories: "the top 20 percent," the "high-performance 70 percent," and "the bottom 10 percent." According to Welch, "the top 20 percent must be loved, nurtured and rewarded in the soul and wallet because they are the ones who make magic happen. Losing one of these people must be held up as a leadership sin." People in the vast middle are encouraged to move up, and there is likely to be movement in and out of the golden 20 percent all the time. "However, the bottom 10 percent, in our experience," says the GE leadership, "tend to remain there." The solution is to determine that 10 percent every year by careful examination of employee performance reports—and remove them.

As dominant as GE is in so many markets, from medical systems to capital services to aircraft engines, Welch was never so arrogant as not to concede that someone else—even another company—might have a brilliant idea. He has publicly acknowledged that GE learned asset management from Toyota, borrowed "Quick Market" intelligence from Wal-Mart, and followed Motorola and Allied Signal's lead, making their "Six Sigma" business model (to deliver quality to customers) so central to GE's successful global business strategy that most managers today think Welch invented it. Nor is Welch afraid to listen to criticism from below. For decades, one of GE's basic management principles was that each one of its businesses had to be number one or two in the marketplace. Then, at one of the regular management training classes, where GE's master black belts coach mid-level executives, students boldly pointed out that this cherished one-or-two share of the market principle had been taken to nonsensical levels. To make their numbers, managers had gradually been redefining their markets more narrowly. Opportunities were missed and growth was limited. "That fresh view shocked us," Welch recalled recently, "and we shocked the system." In the next three-year planning session, Welch informed GE's leaders that they were to redefine their markets so as to have a "10 percent or less share." The result: during the rest of the decade, GE was looking more widely for opportunities for its products and services—and creating double-digit growth rates in revenue.

"What is it that we want to be?" It's the question that every board, CEO, and top manager must ask constantly. The answer constitutes the vision of their company—what today is known as the "mission." Articulating the mission and keeping everyone honest to it is the job of the CEO. You want to be the best company possible, delivering the best and most innovative products to your clients and customers. But any mission will be just a list of empty words unless the Talent Principle is at its center. Only when you promise your customers extraordinary value through extraordinary people will the mission begin to take hold. What separates a great leader from someone who's just an ingenious entrepreneur, a brilliant problem solver, or a wizard salesman is the ability to find talent and use it properly. In the past twenty years, no executive has been praised more for his leadership by the press and his fellow chief executives than Jack Welch. Yet no one has dismissed the idea of CEO as "superman" more than GE's acclaimed super-CEO. "The idea that one person could run a $120 billion company that's in as many businesses as we're in is outrageous on its face," Welch has said. He is very clear about his job description: "My job is selecting people, evaluating people, giving them self-confidence and spreading ideas."

Many CEOs have tried to imitate the management styles and strategies at GE and IBM, with varying success. Granted, it is easier to be Jack Welch and Lew Gerstner with the capital and other resources that glittering brands such as IBM and GE have at their disposal. But any manager in any company can easily imitate their single-minded approach to cultivating talent. We recently worked with a client launching a bold start-up who amazed even us by his commitment to hiring the best talent, no matter the price.

## THE CEO AS CTO—"CHIEF TALENT OFFICER"

A few years ago, we got a call from John Connolly, the founder and CEO of Mainspring, a new Internet company in the Boston area. Connolly's original idea for Mainspring was that it would be a content provider for chief information officers, technology departments, and consulting organizations. Companies that wanted to build Internet-based enterprise systems would be able to go to Mainspring for quick directions to the highest quality local information. Consulting firms, too, would be able to educate themselves about Internet-based enterprise systems in the works and leverage one another's experiences by simply going to Mainspring. But the Internet grew so quickly and Connolly soon noticed that other companies such as razorfish, NerveWire, Scient, and Break Away had already combined their consulting with their systems integration service; worse still, those companies seemed to be way ahead of Mainspring in their technology.

Connolly decided that he didn't want to do what everyone else was doing. He also had reservations about whether high-level business strategy could be fully integrated organizationally with what systems integrators and program analysts do. His solution: a pure play. While his competitors were trying to combine consulting and technology services, Mainspring would go with its strength—strategic consulting to help large companies leverage the Internet. Connolly, however, was not about to limit his ambitions. He wanted Mainspring to become the McKinsey or the Boston Consulting of Internet strategy.

This was a Big Idea. And, frankly, these days the only way you can get the best talent to your company, particularly if it's a start-up or an early-stager, is to have an idea that is so new, so exciting, so edgy, and so salable that the superstars in big positions in major companies looking for a challenge or the opportunity to make a difference cannot resist talking to you. You also need the passion to sell a new idea, and Connolly had a reputation as a born evangelist. He also had a track record, having cofounded Course Technology, Inc., a leading higher education publishing company selling to 3,500 colleges. After Course was acquired by the Thomson Corporation in 1992, Connolly served as president of ITP Media Group, Course, and two other publishing companies within the international Thomson Corporation. Between 1994 and 1996, ITP's revenues went from $40 million to $125 million. He was a businessman who knew how to turn an idea into a company, take it public, and then reward his investors by running a company that made lots of money. Several major venture-capital firms anted up start-up funds.

Connolly quickly lured people away from McKinsey, the Boston Consulting Group, and Bain & Company. He put together an impressive staff of upwards of three hundred people and raised another $35 million. Mainspring was cooking. But Connolly was missing one thing—a member of his executive team who was deeply familiar with strategy consulting and knew the talent in that arena. The investment community was watching carefully; they knew as well as Connolly did that his entire business model was based on the caliber of talent he could get and hold on to. To keep the money people interested, he needed not just a human-resources expert but a top executive with a lot of experience hiring top people who could also help drive the company.

That was our job. And here was our problem: the kind of person Mainspring was looking for did exist, but he was already a partner at places like McKinsey, BCG, Bain, and Booz-Allen. No head-hunter will get rich off the fees of getting people to quit a partner-ship in a billion-dollar organization to join what was basically a start-up. Even if we could get the attention of a partner in an es-tablished consulting firm with Connolly's Big Idea, the money Mainspring had budgeted to pay this new "chief people officer" would present a pay cut of hundreds of thousands of dollars.

Connolly refused to let the compensation issue scare him off. "I want to talk to them anyway," he informed Bob Nephew, the Chris-tian & Timbers partner in the Boston office working with him. I would be lying if I said it was easy to persuade heavy-hitting strat-egy consultants to take Mainspring seriously. But we had Con-nolly's previous successes to point to, we had the investors, and we had the Big Idea. Most of all, we had a CEO pumped by the chal-lenge of sitting down with a candidate who should have been be-yond the reach of such a small company. Nephew rolled up his sleeves and did a miraculous job of persuading people from virtu-ally every marquee strategy consulting firm with human-resources experience to meet with Connolly—from partners who specialized in recruiting talent to those who had merely done a stint in super-vising recruitment for their firms. (Some of the big consulting firms require partners to focus on HR on a rotating basis.) We even delivered the person we thought was perfect for Connolly. His name was Michael Armano.

But here's what we were up against: Armano was in the middle of a great career that could only get better. He had just been made a full partner at the prestigious Boston Consulting Group, and there was an equity play in his near future. Who would leave all that to go to a start-up? Armano refused to take our phone calls. After five calls, he finally agreed to meet Bob Nephew for a half-hour. By the end of the meeting, Armano's curiosity had gotten the best of him; he was willing to listen to Connolly's spiel. Nephew was elated because he knew that it would be hard for Armano to resist Connolly. The Mainspring CEO was notorious among head-hunters for being, as Nephew says, "relentless" in a search. Few CEOs throw themselves into the interviewing process with Connolly's enthusiasm and persistence.

Armano met with Connolly not just once but a second time. "By the time John finished the first two interviews with Armano," recalls Nephew, "he knew everything about the guy, including where his grandparents had come from in Italy. He asked him about his childhood. He found out that he was the kind of person who when he threw out his arm pitching as a kid, he retrained himself to pitch with the other arm. Connolly also learned that Armano was someone who could move up and down the ladder of abstraction. He had the business background and functional strengths we were looking for, and he was a leader to boot." Above all, Armano was the triple threat Mainspring needed: a top manager who had experience in strategic consulting and HR. From the outset, Connolly had set the bar very high, personally directing the search, and when we delivered a perfect match, he was not going to let his original budget get in the way.

Nor was he going to let Armano off the hook. I can't tell you how often we find the right person, and the client backs off because of money or a tough negotiation over other issues. It's amazing how creative you can get when the client is always at your side trying to close the search. Connolly never lost his focus; he was never too busy to make another phone call or take another meeting. A few times during the process, Armano scratched his head and wondered why he was even talking to Mainspring. But Connolly kept talking, and Armano kept listening. One Saturday, they met from eight in the morning to almost two in the afternoon, discussing Armano's goals, working over the financials. "For many companies this would have been the closing meeting, but not for John," recalls Nephew with a laugh as he tells how Connolly called him at home on Saturday night to discuss the meeting. Connolly had gone home afterward, sat down at his desk, and spent the rest of the afternoon writing down what he had learned about Armano—and then read it to Nephew over the phone. "Everything," says Nephew. "He had written about the candidate's strengths, his background, how he could help the company. He also had written a section on why the position was right from Armano's point of view." Meantime, Connolly had his CFO working up a financial scenario with the kind of equity that would assure Armano of Mainspring's seriousness. According to Nephew, "Connolly even got creative about compensating Armano for the amount of money he'd be losing by walking away from his BCG partnership—three times the original figure in his budget."

Connolly was telling all this to Bob Nephew on Saturday night because he wanted to meet with Armano again on Sunday. Nephew called Armano first thing Sunday morning, filled him in, and set up a dinner meeting for that night. By the end of the dinner, Mike Armano said he wanted to help build John Connolly's company. He resigned from BCG to join Mainspring's executive management with the title of senior VP and "chief people officer." The company thrived, going public in July 2000. Eight months later, IBM announced an $80 million deal to acquire the four-year-old Mainspring in an effort to strengthen its own business strategy consulting business. IBM reported it was eager to address the increasing demand for integrated business consulting and information-technology services—John Connolly's Big Idea. But by acquiring Mainspring, IBM was also getting talent it did not have.

That is your number-one goal as a leader: to get as much talent to your side as possible. Of course, you have to know what genuine talent looks like.

## CHAPTER 3

## *Recognizing Talent*

Check this résumé out: *forty-five years old; B.A., Stanford; M.B.A., Harvard; nine years running information technology for a billion-dollar sports-entertainment agency; previously, technology strategy consultant for one of the top three firms in the world.*

Excellent credentials by any measure, and particularly impressive for the job we were looking to fill—senior VP of technology (other companies call it "chief information officer") for a midsize professional services company that happened to be Christian & Timbers. The résumé seemed perfect: professional services background, IT chief for a business ten times bigger than ours, strategic consulting experience, plus a classy educational pedigree. What the résumé implied was also appealing: he had moved up and been generously rewarded. This candidate looked like a winner.

But when one of my colleagues interviewed him, he got a different picture. This large company, it turned out, used a relatively small, in-house technology operation of only fifty-five employees. As head of information technology, he had in fact outsourced all his applications development. For his deployment, he had divided the world into seven geographic organizations with an individual in charge of all IT functions and responsibilities for each geographic area. It was a bit like having a company divided up into seven parts, each run by a division manager who also had financial and sales responsibility for his piece of the action; all the CEO had to do was keep in touch with his division managers. Our candidate had been more of a coach than a hands-on technology chief. We came away from the interview thinking that this was a bright man, fun to talk to, with some interesting notions about strategy and contributions to business, and so on. But he did not fit our needs. In a company as small as ours, the senior VP for technology has to be a hands-on person, an applications developer as well as an applications deployer. Our head of technology could not be a guy sitting at a keyboard all day, and we were certainly not looking for an IT coach. The person we hired would have to be able to figure out how to get technology into the hands of our clients; he would have to be clued in to what was happening in the industry, have his ear to the ground for what the competition was up to, and then be innovative enough to take us to the next level. Our IT chief would also have to be a good recruiter who could bring in and supervise the people key to making it all happen.

Beware of glittering résumés! The great résumé is easy to find; talent is not. In my experience, most executives interview the résumé. It is understandable. You want to evaluate a candidate, and here are all these so-called "objective" standards of measurement and years of preselection staring you in the face. How wrong can Harvard, Stanford, and the HR department of a billion-dollar company be? Don't get me wrong. I am not against Stanford and Harvard per se. They, along with other elite universities and colleges, have produced their share of great business leaders. But a list of prestige schools and blue-chip jobs on a résumé does not always tell the whole story. Middle management throughout America is populated by *countless* alumni of the Ivy League, along with A students from the top B-schools. And most of them will retire as middle managers. Over the years, I have met many successful business people with checkered academic careers. A college dropout myself, I am delighted to take my place among them. At this stage of my career, however, it is not important where I went to school; by now, I have learned things about business that they do not teach in universities. Employers must recognize that talent comes in many forms, and so does education. Your needs as an employer are likely to be different from those of B-school deans of admissions. While they are inclined to choose their students on the basis of college grades and Graduate Record Examinations, you're looking for the right person for a particular job. Brilliance at taking tests will not always correlate to the kind of talent you need to wipe out the competition. Headhunters do not *read* résumés; they *decode* them, looking for evidence of genuine talent.

## DECODING A RÉSUMÉ

If a résumé were a graph, the career path you want is one that keeps rising—no hills and valleys. For me, this is the primary question every résumé must answer: Is this career on an upward trajectory? The people you want do not get hired for a VP job, then move to a lower position at another company as director of whatever, then get hired as VP in the next job. To a headhunter, this says that a candidate is much better at selling himself at a job interview than at doing the job. A résumé, however, with one more important position after another tells me that this person's bosses thought he was talented.

It is not even important how good or bad the companies are. One of the big frustrations for most headhunters is working with a client who is unrealistic, the kind of CEO who thinks that everyone should want to work for his wonderful company, no matter how small or where it might be located. But wizards at Cisco or GE or— you name your favorite great American company—are not likely to want to jump from that kind of luxury liner to a rowboat. My job is to try to persuade CEOs and search committees that diamonds can be found in all sorts of rough companies, even lousy ones. In fact, it is the struggling company that is more likely to throw more and more responsibility to the few people in-house who are delivering. You can see it in their résumés: one, two, three, four promotions in a row within a year or two. Better still, this is the kind of person who is more likely to recognize that he will be unable to grow the company single-handedly (or maybe it's a company whose time has passed or will never come) and after four challenging positions is ready to move on. Talented people are everywhere—if you know what to look for.

## BEYOND THE FIRM HANDSHAKE

No matter how hard we try to be "objective," most of us are inclined to judge people on the basis of first impressions. We humans are wired that way, at least according to recent academic studies about the importance of first impressions. One experiment setting out to discover the nonverbal factors in good teaching revealed that most people could rate the teacher on a fifteen-item checklist of personality traits after viewing *a ten-second silent video clip.* The results were the same even when the researchers showed just two seconds of tape. Snap judgments, according to this study, really are made in a snap—literally within seconds of laying eyes on someone. The study also indicated that the snap judges showed no ambivalence about their evaluations. More amazing still, when the researcher compared those first impressions with teacher evaluations made after a full semester of classes, the correlations were astoundingly high.

In another more recent study, a psychologist used a series of ninety-eight interviews videotaped for another study to test out the old bromide that "the handshake is everything." Taking fifteen seconds of videotape—the interviewee knocks on the door, enters, shakes hands with the interviewer, and sits down—the researcher asked a series of observers to rate the applicants according to the same criteria the actual interviewers had used. "The strength of the correlations were extraordinary," says the researcher. Those who saw only the handshake pretty much predicted the response of the trained interviewers, who had spent upwards of twenty minutes with each candidate.

Of course, that still doesn't mean first impressions are correct.

For while you may make a judgment about someone as soon as he comes through the door, you still cannot be certain how smart he is, or honest, or driven. The person with the strongest handshake in the world could also be a world champion slacker. And how can you determine leadership in two seconds? Some might even argue that you are not likely to learn much more about a complete stranger in forty minutes, the duration of the average job interview. Considering that the person sitting in your office is supposed to be a brilliant salesman, what can you really learn about her in under an hour that she doesn't want you to know?

Some managers are born psychologists; they are natural interviewers of talent. But being a good interviewer is something that you can learn. I pride myself on having a natural feel for people, but I have learned much about interviewing from talented interviewers I have worked with. There is also a huge literature on the subtleties of interviewing; industrial psychology has been an academic specialty for decades. Every search firm has to train its new associates in the art of interviewing. But before we begin teaching our new people about the art and science of interviewing talent we want them to have a clear idea of what talent is. The best way to get there, I think, is to first consider:

## WHAT TALENT IS NOT

### *Talent Is Not Just Filling a Job*

All of us have had staffers who are not cutting it, who are just not as engaged in their work or as productive as others. You haven't fired them because, well, somebody's got to do the job, and you're not even sure that you could find *anyone* to replace them, never mind someone who actually might be better. Now try to remember what it was like when you actually hired this person. Why did you do it? What inspired you? My bet is that he wasn't the best available candidate who walked through the door at the time; moreover, he was probably better at being interviewed than at managing. I would also bet that you didn't have much of a choice. If so, that means your talent pipeline was weak. Hiring talent is not simply getting a warm body behind a desk as fast as you can.

### Talent Is Not Just Skill

Talented people are skilled, but not all skilled people are talented. Most people can learn a skill, whether it's furniture making, playing the violin, operating a computer, or selling products. I have always been pretty good at one-on-one communication. Speaking before an audience, however, was another matter. The bigger the group I had to address, the more petrified I was. And in front of a television camera—well, let's just say that afterward I felt happy to be alive. As I do more TV and public speaking, I can feel myself getting more comfortable at it, more skilled. Will I ever turn into Ronald Reagan or Bill Clinton? I doubt it, because they are talented communicators.

### Talent Is Not About Perfection

If you snag the Mozart of marketing or computer programming, you are a lucky duck. But you do not set out to get Mozart. It is amazing how many clients come to me expecting me to lure stars away from Microsoft or IBM to their less-celebrated shops. Why would those people leave one of the most successful companies in the history of capitalism to come to work for you? If you have a good answer to that question, terrific. Let's talk. But if your answer is what I think it is, my advice is: "Get real!" You are more likely to be successful in your talent hunt if your wish list is realistic.

## Talent Is Not Even About Experience

One of the easiest (and biggest) mistakes bosses make is to look for someone who's done the job before. On the face of it, such a strategy makes perfect sense: you need a head of marketing, and this candidate has been head of marketing for five years, and for a company bigger than yours. It seems like a no-brainer. Unfortunately, such a decision fails to address one crucial question: If this candidate is so talented, why is she still only VP of marketing? And why does she want to leave such a great company for a lateral (or maybe even a downward) move to your shop?

## Talent Has Nothing to Do with Gender or Skin Color or Nationality

The numbers are not exactly inspiring. As I write, there are five female CEOs of Fortune 500 companies—HP's Carly Fiorina, Xerox's Anne Mulcahy, Avon's Andrea Jung, Cinda A. Hallman of Spherion Corporation (a company that supplies temporary staffers), and Golden West Financial Corporation's Marion O. Sandler. Only 12.5 percent of the corporate officers in the Fortune 500 are women—1,622 out of 12,945—and of the top earners at those companies, only 4.1 percent are female. Ninety companies (18 percent of the Fortune 500) reported zero women among their top ranks. In a poll of 400 companies, Catalyst, an organization that tracks women in business, found that women of color accounted for a mere 1.3 percent of the corporate officers. African-American men and other people of color aren't exactly taking over the executive suite, either. In 2000, there were two black Fortune 500 CEOs—Franklin Raines, a former investment banker and member of the Clinton administration who runs Fannie Mae, and Lloyd Ward, a former top executive at Procter & Gamble and PepsiCo before he became Maytag's chief executive in 1999. Fifteen months later, after what the press called a "stormy" reign, Ward was out, resurfacing as CEO of iMotors, a start-up on-line car seller, leaving Raines as the only African-American chief executive in the Fortune 500. The number of African-Americans at the top of U.S. business went back up to two in January 2001, when Kenneth Chenault, forty-nine, who had been president and COO of American Express, succeeded Harvey Golub as AMEX's CEO. Golub stepped down as chairman in March, and the board immediately handed the title over to CEO Chenault, a talented marketer who had helped Golub revive the American Express brand and was his choice as a successor. Then in December, AOL Time Warner's Gerald Levin surprised Wall Street by announcing he was stepping down. His successor would be his right-hand man, AOL Time Warner's president and former aide to Vice President Nelson Rockefeller, Richard Parsons, fifty-three.

Five hundred companies, five women and three African-American men at the helm.

This is a big problem. Corporate America remains a society dominated by white men. But it is a problem, I believe, that the most successful companies are now in the process of solving by hiring women and minorities—and not just because it is the right thing to do (which it is) but because it is the most realistic, rational, and forward-looking business strategy. And while the number of women in chief executive roles is still minuscule, our database and personal networks feature scores of talented women ready to move to the CEO level. Over the past twenty years, women have gradually moved up the corporate pyramid, getting experience in every area of their companies, solving problems, getting promoted. Anyone who still doubts how good women can be in business should spend some time studying *Fortune*'s list of the "50 Most Powerful Women in Business." Number one in 2001—for the fourth year in a row—was HP's Carly Fiorina, the only woman to run a company in *Fortune*'s top twenty. But number two was Meg Whitman, CEO of eBay, the on-line auction house that is not only making an impressive profit ($129 million on revenues of $740 million) but also is growing 72 percent a year. In addition to repeats such as Fiorina, Jung, and Oprah, the list included impressive talent from such major players as Pfizer, Chevron, Kraft Foods, Ford, PepsiCo, and Colgate-Palmolive. Is there anyone out there who can say with a straight face that they wouldn't want executives like this on their team?

This is the future. And while other industries, such as financial services and manufacturing may still be lagging behind the techs, they will be forced to catch up, if only by the realities of the market for talented business leaders. Today, women make up the majority of law students, and at least 40 percent of the MBA degrees awarded in recent years went to women. Are there companies really ready to ignore almost half of the graduating attorneys and MBAs just because they are inexperienced or uncomfortable working with women? As the pool of talent gets smaller, companies will be forced to expand their choices through diversity. It is already happening. Our firm's requests from clients for women and minority candidates for top positions have increased by 32 percent this year alone.

The prospects for African-Americans and Hispanics are more complicated. Even companies eager to hire minorities cannot find enough candidates. The very best of these candidates have their pick of the available jobs. While the current pool of minorities remains small, the evidence on the streets of our inner cities of potential business talent—entrepreneurial genius, type-A behavior, passion, drive, and leadership—is undeniable. But for too many young people in the inner cities, a big job in the business world seems as remote as a trip to Venus. They need to see role models. Business leaders must visit urban schools, create special programs, invest in more scholarships that will prove to young minority kids that the dream of having a big job in business is not a fantasy but a simple reality of the Talent Economy.

You cannot win without talent, and these days talent comes in all varieties. Talent, as I have also stressed, is attracted to talent. It flourishes in an open culture that encourages creativity and innovation, in companies that allow people to do what they're good at. When today's smart, young executives arrive at your company for an interview, they will be looking for evidence of all of the above. If they see only a bunch of middle-aged white guys, that will be a strike against you. Avoiding diversity is simply a bad business strategy. Women spend 80 percent of every consumer dollar in the United States. Doesn't it make sense to have some women in top management to help you work through the sales and marketing strategies for tapping into that market? If women live longer and end up with as much as 90 percent of the wealth (depending on which studies you believe), then shouldn't you have women managers on your side who might help you appeal to the people holding the purse strings? African-Americans and Hispanics spent a total of more than $800 billion last year. Surely it makes sense to have some black and Latino voices in the room; they have some good ideas about how your company can tap into those growing markets. Magic Johnson, the former Los Angeles Lakers basketball star, has opened up a chain of movie theaters in African-American neighborhoods in Los Angeles and New York that have been huge successes at a time when other large cinema chains are hanging on for dear life. Johnson knew his market. He persuaded Starbucks to open a café in his movie complex in L.A.'s notorious South Central area—and it's become one of the most successful Starbucks in the city. One reason: Johnson convinced Starbucks to stock snacks and sweets that appealed specifically to African-American tastes (sweet potato pie, for example). Another reason: people in the area did not have a place to congregate or to meet their kids after school. Magic knew his customers in a way that the Starbucks marketing people in Seattle never could. Starbucks listened, and everyone benefited.

The face of America is getting browner and more Asian (the fastest-growing market in America). Any American who thinks immigration is a thing of the past has not visited a public school lately. According to the latest census figures, nearly one in ten people living in the United States today was born in another country. The dominance of the white person has been history in New York City and Houston for years; as of 2001, whites are in the minority in the entire state of California. In race and ethnicity, as in so many other things, California is the future. Fifty years from now, there will be no racial majority in America. All those different ethnic groups are your customers. Nor is the reality of diversity limited to consumer products. In today's America, virtually every customer base is a mosaic of colors and ethnic identities. If you sell financial services or software, machine tools or plastics, tape measures or duct tape, the people who buy all these things are from a variety of backgrounds. The more people on your team who understand these customers, the more successful your company will be. We advise our clients to hire people who are different than they are. It is a strategy we believe adds a fresh point of view, creativity, and growth to a management team.

In my experience, reactions against women or minorities are due less to outright prejudice than to some people's discomfort in the face of difference. I remember interviewing a successful woman years ago for a job and being disarmed by how incredibly tough and bottom-line-driven she was. I still catch myself taking particular notice when a woman I am interviewing seems more ambitious, tougher, and caustic than the men I've talked to. We tend to prefer what we know, what we are comfortable with. Businessmen of a certain age have been working almost exclusively with white men their entire lives. How do you react to a black woman? How to handle not one difference but two? Do you treat black women differently?

Whenever people raise such questions with me, I have a simple answer: Just treat her the same way you would any valued employee, which better be with respect and gratitude. Otherwise you will lose her to the competition.

## WHAT IS TALENT?

I often ask the CEOs I interview what their take on talent is. Businesspeople tend to be dazzled by the successful entrepreneur.

It is not surprising. As the people who literally create a business out of nothing, entrepreneurs are the true *artists* of the marketplace. They dream up new ideas and imagine companies to turn those ideas into products, technologies, or services; they find financing for these companies, grow them, and drive them faster and faster. I see this over and over in my clients who have actually invented businesses. I worked with Ken Tuchman, the founder-chairman of TeleTech, a Denver-based outsourcing company that Tuchman took from less than zero to $350 million. TeleTech is now the leading provider in the world of customer relations management services and solutions for large companies around the world. Like many smart people, Tuchman is able to access from his memory at any moment the details of one of the many different deals he has going as well as a particular name from the myriad of relationships he has built. He is also one of those people who works constantly on multiple levels, paying attention to what is happening in every area of his company and business strategy. He knows what the technology is and what his customers want. And if he's not sure on either count, he's on an airplane to go find the answer. Ken Tuchman is always hiring and thinking about whom else to hire. He exudes such passion and fire for his business that other good people want to be close to his flame. But as talented as he is, he also knows he is an outside guy, a salesman who needs operational backup—and he hires those people to help him. Watching Tuchman in action, it is not difficult to understand how he became a billionaire before he was forty.

Great entrepreneurs like Tuchman are the tightrope walkers of the marketplace, and the rest of us just look up in awe. Such superstars, of course, are not about to work for you. But they are exemplars of talent. Study them, and search for people who remind you of them—smart, energetic, passionate people like Tuchman who build industries and fortunes . . . and careers.

In big companies, according to my sources, the most talented people are typically those who get thrown into the worst situations time and time again and turn things around. They are problem solvers. The word is: "Joe knows how to make things happen, so let's give him this bad region or this troubled division." And Joe succeeds. You are probably no more likely to get your hands on Joe than on a great entrepreneur because most companies keep their Joes very happy and well compensated. But you definitely want to be looking for problem solvers who might be dissatisfied with their current position or who are looking for new challenges. And you should definitely be looking for a young Joe.

The simplest way for me to nail down the kind of managers I'm looking for as a headhunter is to draw an analogy to baseball: you want to find the people who are batting as close to a thousand as possible. You want to find the people working for successful companies who are knocking the ball out of the park in their specialties. You want to hire the best catcher, the best pitcher, the best outfielder who can also hit the long ball. One of the reasons I like sports analogies is that sports, like business, is not only competitive but you can also win in many different ways. The best product or technology, for example, does not always capture the market. In the arts, or medicine, or the other sciences, we expect a kind of perfection from the top practitioners. A talented cardiologist does not bat .300, and the same goes for great violinists and writers. In baseball, however, you can earn iconic status by doing the job less than half the time. Only six players in the history of the game have had one-year batting averages over .400. The most recent was Ted

Williams, who hit .406 in 1941. But even though the most talented hitters cannot be expected to get a hit every time at bat, they are a threat every time. Same in business.

How can you put yourself in a position of increasing your chances to get the very best? When I am training the young head-hunters at my own firm, I tell them that they have to find bench-marks: compare new interviewees to the best people they have interviewed in the past. Every time you go into an interview, you have to have a picture of the complete executive in your mind. In our company that picture has been institutionalized in the Formula Five: (1) Honesty and Integrity; (2) Intellectual Firepower; (3) Energy and Passion; (4) Leadership; (5) Humility. That is the gold standard, and you may not think you can afford the price. But exceptional leaders are what talented people become. Your challenge is to find talent before others do, early in their career, when they still come cheap. To accomplish that, you have to be on the lookout for evidence that a young manager is a potential Formula Five. Here are the signs:

### Talent Is Someone on the Way Up

The résumé, as we saw, will be the first tip. Checking references carefully will confirm that this is really a career in the middle of its trajectory, with potential to burn. The earlier you can detect such potential, the better chance you will have of hiring a star before the competition. Then you want to promote this manager. Again and again. Warning: real talent can move at blazing speed, so when you see it, grab it. Don't risk waiting for a person to mature. Case in point: when I began writing this chapter, Tiger Woods (sticking to my sports analogy) was a young athlete whose trajectory was on the rise. A few months later, when I returned to revise this section, Tiger Woods had won six out of his last thirteen tournaments, including wiping out his opposition to win the U.S. and British Opens, completing the Grand Slam of golf at twenty-four, all within three years of turning pro. When I reread it again, after another month, Woods had won the PGA, another international title (earning $2 million in prize money in two weeks), and a few weeks after that the Canadian Open. This is a trajectory so steep that in a matter of months Woods's résumé went from "phenom" to "one of the all-time greats."

Woods is one of the greatest success stories in sports, but the history of business is full of Tiger Woodses. When you see one, reach for your checkbook. (Which, come to think of it, is exactly what Nike did the day the kid turned pro, offering him a $40 million contract, which many denounced as premature and ludicrous but now seems like an amazing bargain. As I am writing this, they just renewed the contract—for $85 million.)

### *Talent Is Someone You Instantly Feel Good Being Around*

Talented people make you feel smarter and stronger. With such people at your side, you feel you can conquer the world.

### *Talent Is the Person You Particularly Want to Have Around When Things Go Bad*

How hard can it be selling for General Electric or IBM? But when you're up against it, when the you-know-what hits the fan, there are certain people on your team you know you can depend on. You

want more of those people on your team—because they help define "talent."

### *Talent Feels Lucky*

Nothing is going to stop them because they know nothing can.
They emit self-confidence, and that kind of spirit tends to be contagious.

### *Talent Likes to Win*

They are very competitive. There is a reason we call the most talented people in business "winners." Business is about beating the
competition, and the people you want to hire relish the challenge
of a good fight.

### *Talent Is Impatient*

They tend to be "type-A" personalities, intense, driven. They're not
about to sit around waiting for another research report or blue rib-
bon panel to tell them what to think.

### *Talent Gets to the Point*

They stick to the facts, do their homework, and say what has to be
said, concisely and clearly. The people who like to blather do so because they are not quite sure what to think. Talent thinks things
through before they speak.

### Talent Is Likely to Speak Their Mind

The people you are looking for come to meetings well prepared and ask great questions. And you can ask them questions because they have a strategy.

### Talent Has Vision

They can see into the future.

### Talent Brings Other People Into Their Vision

They can articulate their vision—and keep rearticulating it—in such a way that other people want to be part of their team.

### Talent Attracts Other Talent

Look for the person everyone wants to work for. You have noticed those people throughout your own career. If you are lucky, you are one of them. Talent inspires teams, and inspired people are what business success is made of.

### Talent Is Capable of Reinventing the Wheel

Talent does not take the conventional route; it looks at problems sideways. Sometimes talent looks like a troublemaker, which is why it takes a smart, experienced, and talented leader to distinguish the bad apples from the winners.

## *Talent Is a Strategic Thinker and a Good Listener*

Strategic thinkers listen to their colleagues, their customers, and their competition—and after assimilating all that information, they make a decision. Good listeners know when to stop listening and take action.

## *Talent Will Surprise You*

This is one of the qualities I am always looking for. After thousands of interviews, I have heard it all. And then someone will surprise me with a question or a comment or a story. Suddenly, I am listening more carefully and placing this candidate at the top of my list.

## *Talent Is Your "Special Sauce"*

It's what separates you from the rest. Talent, in fact, is so valuable to your firm that:

## *Talent Is Someone Who Might Even Replace You*

I have set the standards of talent quite high, and at this point you might wonder whether you yourself are talented. After all, you are a rational person, you pride yourself on being a practical business strategist, and although you are, all things considered, a pretty smart dude (you may even have risen to general manager, or even CEO), you have accepted the fact that you are no Jack Welch or John Chambers. If you're a young person planning a career, you may be getting nervous now, wondering whether you bought the wrong book. Smart though you may be, packed with ambition to spare and willing to work until you drop, you are not a genius.

Relax. The business and sports careers I have cited are likely the products of genius. But the genius is someone who is extremely talented, indeed, divinely so. Most of us are definitely not in their league, and since most of us actually run the world (and hire the Jack Welches and Michael Jordans), we have to put genius into perspective, on a scale of one to ten. We can also enjoy the important fact that you can make a lot of money with people who are way short of a perfect ten. Because:

### Talent Is Relative

None of us operates in a vacuum. Everything we do, including our success, *depends* on our resources, on our competition, on the marketplace, on circumstances, on the economy, not to mention a little bit of luck. Every business has its own unique needs, and those needs may differ over time. I often interview candidates who are not the right people. But when I consider the specific needs of a particular company at a unique moment in time, an imperfect candidate may be absolutely perfect. For example: one of my colleagues recently interviewed someone for a CFO position who asked very good and important questions. Trouble was, he also asked a lot of trivial and irrelevant questions, even as the interview was winding down. And he was not winging it; throughout the interview, he kept referring to a list of prepared questions. The headhunter inferred from this performance that not only was the candidate extremely detail oriented, he was obviously not the kind of manager who was able to set priorities. Frankly, this was the kind of manager who would drive a less detail-oriented boss crazy within two years. But . . . if your company is in a mess and needs to be reorganized fast—say, within two years—this person may be your CFO.

### Talent Is Your Own Value in the Marketplace

Let's face it: people talk behind our backs. We all develop a reputation, whether in the context of our own company or within an industry. You want to control and manage your reputation as much as possible. And you can.

"Jeff Christian is a good guy." That's clearly a plus, and there's plenty of things you can do to make sure that your colleagues, bosses, and underlings do not assert otherwise. "Christian is a good guy, *but . . .*" Here's where the problems arise, after that "but": he isn't smart enough, or doesn't work hard enough, or speak his mind, or take chances, or he's too tough on people. Thus, while a huge dose of talent might be innate, it is up to us to make sure that when people talk about our performances, there are as few "buts" as possible.

As you can see, talent is many things. Above all, searching for talent is about defining a standard for your situation, for your business, for your division, for your department. To do that, it helps to analyze your company just as a headhunter would.

## THINKING LIKE A HEADHUNTER ABOUT TALENT

To tailor a talent search for different clients, the headhunters in my firm ask variations of the following questions.

- What specifically are you looking for in a candidate?
- Would you prefer someone with lots of experience or great potential?
- Who's the best person who left recently?
- What was it about that employee that you loved, that made him or her a star performer?
- Who's the person in your organization who comes the closest to filling the job—and what is he or she missing?

Write down the answers. The next step is finding out who is available for the job and if they fit your bill of particulars. As we have seen, a résumé is the place to start. But the crucial step is the job interview.

## CHAPTER 4

## *The Interview*

The candidate steps through the door, gives you a smile that blinds you with promise, shakes your hand (firmly, of course), and sits down for the interview. You have analyzed his résumé, made a few calls. He has all the markings of a winner. You have already spoken with him over the phone. First impression: very good. Okay—you now have an hour to find out if the person you are hiring is genuinely as smart, energetic, passionate, creative, humble, and experienced as his résumé and telephone skills suggest.

Oh, one other thing: the job you are filling is vice president of *sales.* How do you separate the sales manager from sales pitch? It is a cliché of business life that you must be your own best salesman. It is also Headhunting 101 that you must make sure that a job candidate is capable of selling more than himself. (Sometimes, you will run into someone who is masquerading as an aspiring VP of sales but whose core skill is really engineering or finance. Is the candidate selling one skill while she excels in another?) It is here that you must strip off the mask of the "promising candidate" to find the real promise inside. To accomplish this, you have to be part Columbo and part Sigmund Freud.

But relax, you can learn how to be a good interviewer. Some people are natural psychologists. They have perfect pitch in the presence of other people and seem to be able to read their minds and connect with their emotions. Such sensitivity, the psychologists now tell us, is a kind of intelligence—*emotional* intelligence. It, too, can be learned. Interviewing is mainly what headhunters do. We talk about interviewing techniques and exchange stories about what goes on in interviews all the time. We also teach our young associates how to become better interviewers. As my partner Steve Mader puts it: "You will not be good at interviewing if you do not have an interest in what makes people tick, if you don't care about how they think and wonder why they do what they do. You must be interested in what creates a successful leader in an organization."

Interviewing is part art, part science. Comparative analysis forms the basis of my own interviewing technique—I'm constantly comparing the candidate's answer to her previous answers, as well as to the answers of the best people I've interviewed in the past. After more than two decades of interviewing people, I've adapted basic comparative analysis to my own personal style. I suppose if someone watched me interview candidates, the logic of what I'm doing might seem elusive. But when you've done literally thousands of interviews, as I have, you are allowed to improvise, according to the assignment, the candidate, and so on; you also go with your gut. (That's the art of it.) Not all headhunters interview the same way. I jump into the middle of my interviews, for example, and sometimes have to resist being too intuitive. Steve Mader, one of the best interviewers I know, has a quieter, more "linear" style. It's really a personality difference, and you will find yourself varying questions according to your own personality and comfort level in one-on-one situations. For those of you who are just starting out or are looking to improve your skills, I suggest you create a plan and stick to it. As you get better and have interviewed more people, you can depend increasingly on your intuition and improvise.

The basic requirements for a successful interview are careful preparation and asking a series of questions that probe deeper and deeper into the candidate's personality and experience. The goal is to find out how good this person is at making decisions and solving problems. The résumé and references indicate that the candidate might be a talented manager. It is now time to find out if she really *is* a talented manager. Consider the interview a window into the candidate's mind. You were curious enough to want to meet this person. Now you have to see if there's a real thinker and doer inside.

## I. THE PRELIMINARIES

To succeed at interviewing, you have to know what your goals are. An interview is just a series of questions and answers. It is the *aim* of the interview that shapes it and makes it worth your time. My aim is to find people brighter than I am, exceptional and experienced managers who can communicate to me complex business concepts and models that are hard for me to understand. The best leaders will make it easier, and that's important to me. The overriding talent I am searching for in a manager is the ability to sift through complex, difficult problems and synthesize the kind of clear-cut plans and initiatives that make companies successful. I want to find out how they make decisions; I want to see them thinking; I want to see the methodology of thought, decision making, and execution that they have developed during their careers.

Mainly, I'm looking for my Formula Five traits—integrity, intellect, drive, leadership ability, and humility—all of which shine through in the course of a good interview. Very smart people are able to explain complicated things clearly and concisely. They don't waste words or time. When they talk about their work and ideas, their passion boils over. You cannot fake enthusiasm (at least in my presence). The better candidates tend to be entertaining; they like to tell stories. This anecdotal style indicates how relaxed they are, how confident they are about themselves. The best leaders I know say things like: "I came into this organization, I listened to the people working there, and I listened to our customers. I found out what we were doing and should be doing. I stopped what we shouldn't be doing, encouraged what we should. I got rid of the people that were getting in the way or holding us back. I got the right people in the right jobs, and let them run. My job was keeping them focused, accountable, and inspired to grow our business and make the organization successful. It is a team effort. I am definitely the leader, the buck stops with me, but we are in it together."

That's what I want every interviewee to say to me, more or less. But don't be too hasty about rejecting someone who is short on flash. The interview is the time to go deep into a candidate's experiences and character. I am a great believer in gut reactions about people, but don't let a snap judgment cause you to miss out on talent that happens to be a little shy or not as smooth a talker as you're used to. GE's Jack Welch is a lifelong stutterer, while Cisco's John Chambers had to contend with the insecurities (and prejudices) that accompany severe dyslexia. Real talent usually lies below the surface.

The job interview is essential for finding and recruiting exceptional talent. I advise my clients to view such interviews as important as anything they do in business. Most businesspeople believe that winning new customers is their most important task. And while it is true that without customers your company does not exist, it is talented salesmanship that brings in customers. Would you dare winging it in a meeting to romance new business? Treat job interviews the same way. Be prepared. How much of your time do you devote to winning new business? Twenty-five percent? A third? Half? You should devote as much time to recruiting and interviewing talent.

*Reference Checks*

Whenever someone asks me if there is a single factor that will guarantee a great hire, my answer is: careful reference checking. After studying a résumé, looking for the upward trends or inconsistencies, I typically check a reference or two or make a phone call to someone I know (or who have interviewed in the past) who might have worked with the person I'm sizing up. We encourage our clients to do most of the reference checking. It is important for them to talk to people who know the candidate.

So, job seekers beware: the best companies will call the names you list as your references—and find even more names. Since it is human nature to give references that will be complimentary, it is in the skeptical nature of headhunters to use those names and companies to get other names—and others, until we find all the references that we need to be effective. "We want two more peers from this company," a headhunter will say. "A subordinate from that company, a board member from this company." The candidate's eagerness or reluctance to give you a name is in itself revealing. If I know people who happen to know a candidate, I will ask the candidate what he thinks that person will say about him. It will also encourage the candidate to discuss his weaknesses honestly because he knows I have access to a former boss or colleague. While the candidate wants us to talk to people who will praise him, a headhunter is eager to get on the phone with a boss or colleague who might bury him, or at least be honest about what business skills the candidate needs to work on. If someone you trust warns you off a candidate, you have saved yourself a lot of time for the price of a phone call.

I recommend that clients meet with a reference in person. My best clients not only do that, they can be very clever at it (others might say sneaky-good). The primary goal is to get an honest evaluation from a reference, and one way to get it is to avoid interrogating them. Engage them in a conversation about their own work and how the candidate fits into that. You want to hear positive things, but I have always found that when pressed, people will confirm or strengthen the validity of a positive comment with an equally strong negative. "She's a great team player," a reference will say. But in my experience, genuine team players are typically slow to make decisions. Another common problem among managers with team-oriented personalities: they are slow to pull the trigger on people who should be fired. Recently, I did a reference check in which my source confirmed that the candidate was smart, focused, and driven. I waited for the "but," and it came. "But," my source confided, "he is probably better big-company material." The reference's company, of course, was a small one. That was a useful conversation: I believed the candidate was really smart and driven *because* this colleague had a strong criticism to add—one that actually confirmed things other references had told me. "He did not engage his organization well," as someone else I checked with had kindly put it. In other words, my candidate was not a team player. Other candidates might have reputations as problem solvers, people who get things done. Two definite signs of talent, as we have seen. The typical criticism for such real performers is that they can be "tough" and "demanding." They make things happen, beat their numbers, but in the course of succeeding, they break a lot of glass. To a headhunter, such descriptions mean that this executive does not "manage up" well. They get things done and protect the organization, but they do not engage their superiors. They also tend to be secretive.

Another way to squeeze some criticisms out of your sources is to play to their egos. "I see you are quite impressed by what a good person and team player this candidate is. What would you coach them on?" That usually inspires an honest evaluation of your candidate: they will tell you that this nice guy should work on his energy or intensity to get things done. You can also call a reference you know and, to keep things confidential, say, "I'm looking to fill a job. Someone told me about Jim Mitchell. Is he worth calling?" If your confidant is complimentary and knows something about the candidate, you should ask for possible areas to focus on. Sometimes you might have to be careful. You're fishing for candidates in a small pool, after all. A reference might know a candidate's current boss and alert him that this person is thinking of quitting. Or your own interest in a particular manager might perk up someone else's. Why spark a bidding war? To mask my interest in a candidate, one trick that I often use is to prepare a list of five or six people from different companies, along with the candidate I'm most interested in. I then call my source with the following request: "I'm in the middle of a search and have been given the names of six people you know. How would you rank them?"

Effective reference checking will generate plenty of information to help you prepare interview questions. I would advise making at least ten to twelve phone calls. Even if the candidate turns out to be a loser whom you do not want to interview, the phone calls are likely to turn up other recommendations. But before you interview any candidate for the job, you must know exactly what kind of manager you are looking for. That, in turn, requires being realistic about your company, a difficult task. I would advise that you try to forget it is your company and try to view it objectively—as a headhunter might.

### *Evaluate Your Company Like a Headhunter*

I encourage the young headhunters in my firm to have a clear sense of the client's needs. That requires spending some time trying to understand the client's business and the concerns unique to it. Of course, you already know your own business inside out. Amazingly, however, many employers spend too much time in interviews on general questions or ones related to the business a candidate is in instead of focusing the interview on their own business goals. The thought that ought to hang over your interview like a flashing neon sign is: *How will this candidate's experience and soft skills fit with my needs?* Make sure you are absolutely clear on what those needs are. Too often I see clients who have a fantasy in mind:

they want to start a new division, or a new business, and they hire someone to do that—and then discover that they cannot really afford to take a chance on something new. The result is one very disappointed (and high-priced) new manager.

While you may know your business, you might be a bit sketchy on what some positions actually entail. Often a CEO or hiring manager with a scientific or technical background is not as sophisticated about the nuances of marketing or distribution or manufacturing. You better be sure what the job is you're looking to fill. If you are not, ask around, talk to experts, do your homework. With every candidate you consider, you must ask yourself: How will this person make an impact on my company? Will he or she improve my bench strength and make us a stronger organization? This will help you avoid interviewing the wrong person. For example: Are you looking for someone to transform your organization? Or is your goal to turn it around totally? If you're looking for someone with real depth in understanding of your product, then you might not want to be talking to candidates who have never been in your business. But if you need a fresh eye, perhaps a brilliant, hard-driving manager from another industry is the spoon you need to stir things up in your organization.

A big chunk of any headhunter's time is spent trying to persuade talented candidates to meet with the client. Clients tend to think that everyone ought to want to work for their company; some even resent resistance on the part of the candidate and strike the ingrate off their shortlist. Talented managers will have many good companies to choose from. To make the best case for your company, a headhunter will look at it with a cold eye; you should do the same. Here are some suggestions to encourage your objectivity:

**Become familiar with your prime sources of talent.** Headhunters look for a transition that is the easiest for all sides. Talent from certain kinds of companies or specific companies might be a good fit for your own. Know which ones they are. Indeed, you ought to try to know the companies in your business or area so well that you not only know the names of who is doing what in each company but you are also able to conjure up the actual conditions a given prospect might be working under—and make sure you are offering him a more attractive (and lucrative) alternative. Search firms like mine have long lists of managers from every kind of company. If you're looking for a head of marketing in a major Internet firm, you should know who's available at eBay or Juniper Networks. If you're in the retail-consumer products business, who is good at companies such as Wal-Mart, Nike, Starbucks? If software's your game, what is your dream team, based on talent from the software companies you admire most? Also familiarize yourself with nearby companies, so that a potential hire does not have to move his family across the country to get to you. For certain candidates, your firm might be a closer commute than her current position. You want to have that information.

**Be prepared to go outside your industry.** One obstacle I run into constantly is that my clients insist on hiring from within the same industry. It can be a huge mistake. Why not hire someone who is just plain talented? Believe me, in six to eight months a talented marketing person, or manager, or strategist, will be able to learn everything there is to know about your business—and then there's the bonus that your new executive is actually talented. IBM's Lew Gerstner came from RJR Nabisco. Home Depot recently filled their

CEO position with the head of GE Power Systems, Robert Nardelli, whose name had been mentioned as a possible successor to Jack Welch. Another loser in the Jack Welch sweepstakes, GE Aircraft Engines boss James McNerney, Jr., won the big job at 3M. Did IBM worry whether Gerstner would be able to switch from selling cookies to computers? Did Home Depot test Nardelli's skill with a jigsaw or hanging a screen door?

**Put yourself in the candidate's shoes.** It is very important to ask yourself: *Why would someone as good as that want to join my company?* The answer will help make your expectations reasonable or provide ideas to improve your company. And don't expect young managers to sign on for the same reason you did years ago. People tend to change jobs for one of three reasons: (1) They want a more exciting job; (2) they want a bigger job; (3) they want more money. Know what the candidates you're interviewing are looking for, and deliver it. Even if it takes 40 percent more money than you're used to paying for a particular job position, talent will make up the difference in productivity.

**Evaluate yourself against the competition.** What might *they* do to attract someone as good as that? If another company would give the person a bigger job or a better title or even more support staff, then maybe you should be considering those alternatives, too. Know thy enemy. Grill your customers about who among the people working for the competition they are most impressed with. This will provide you with a useful standard for gauging the candidate—as well as another source of possible people to recruit. If you do not have a major competitor, imagine one that would have the best talent in every job. Now analyze what those "must-haves" are. The results are what you should be looking for in your next hires.

**Be aware of what the competition (or ex-employees) will say about you.** I like to ask my clients what we are likely to hear about their companies in the course of our recruiting. If a potential candidate is going to slam a company, we want to be prepared with our reply. You also have to be clear on what your company's biggest selling points are. It is amazing how many clients will say, "It's a fun place to work," or "It's a nonpolitical environment." You must be more self-conscious about your company than that. In fact, you must be brutal. Unless there are obvious reasons for someone to work for you, no one will want to. If you do not know your strengths, how will you be able to sell your company effectively to prospective candidates? And if you do not know the criticisms of your company, then you will not know how to turn it into the kind of place where talent will want to work. Companies tend to ignore their failings. But when your stock price goes down, it is exactly *those* defects that the headhunters working for the competition will be stressing during their phone calls to your best people.

**Contemplate who the best person for this job might be—and take some risks.** Every position has its own unique needs. A manager, for instance, who will be meeting with your top clients will have to be presentable. However, a wizard Java programmer featuring green hair and body piercings might not be the person you introduce to your most conservative client. (Then again, he might be. In today's Internet world, you might end up wheeling out your weirdest techie as proof of how innovative and open to risks you are as a company.) Companies, particularly emerging growth ones, are full of all sorts of different kinds of talent—thinkers, doers, mavericks, strategists. You have to take some chances. Think back on your own career; try to recall why someone gave you a break early on that helped you rise quickly in the organization or your career. Why did they take a chance on you? The answer should be applied to your next hire. Trust your gut, and go for it.

**Which candidate do you want to be in the trenches with?** I learned this from the venture capitalist John Doerr, who told me that sometimes he looks at a candidate and wonders whether he'd want to be with this person when it really hits the fan. I think it's an equally useful way for anyone in a position of recruiting talent to evaluate managers. Let's face it, even the most woodenheaded executive can look good when business is great. But when you're losing money, when the competition is beating the hell out of you, who is it that you want to have next to you, fighting back? It is a question that should remain in the back of your mind throughout the interview process.

**Don't compromise on the Formula Five.** Companies tend to demand experience and compromise on things that are not easy to learn, such as personality or passion. For a headhunter, however, potential is always more important than experience. I prefer looking for an up-and-comer who may be short on experience but loaded with the right personality traits.

## *Prepare Specific Questions and Expect Specific Answers*

When training our young recruiters, we warn them about hypothetical answers, the kind you can get away with in a business school classroom. Talent is in the details. Often in interviews, when you ask somebody a question about a specific situation they faced in their current job, they say, "Well, what I would do is . . ." or "What should be done is . . ." Our people are trained to stop them right there, put them at ease by saying that maybe they weren't clear enough. "What I'm looking for," you must explain, "is a specific example from a specific situation you found yourself in." Real life. Only then will you get the kind of detail and clarity that will convince you that this person was actually there. Only then will you get a sense of whether this candidate has the kind of mind and decision-making skills you're looking for.

Maybe you have to fill the position of chief financial officer. The résumé sitting on your desk says this guy has been CFO for a public company for three years. How has the company's stock done? In any given period some companies are highly valued on Wall Street. Some good companies can't seem to wake up the market. That's the CFO's job, and you should be prepared to ask him about his relations with Wall Street.

Warning: while you want details, too much detail, too much talk or explanation, signals quite the opposite kind of mind you are trolling for. Blatherers don't mind wasting time with talk. The kind of person you're looking for is focused, concise, says what needs to be said, and moves on to the next problem at hand.

*Real Talent Will Not Take Your Call (at Least Not the First Time)*

Be wary of people too eager for a new job. When someone is looking too hard for a position, my skepticism meter rises: Why is he so eager to leave? Is it because he's being squeezed out—or wants to leave before he is asked to go? As we have seen, talent generally rises up through the ranks. Things are going great. She's thinking about the next promotion, not about leaving. The person I'm inclined to like does not even want to talk to a headhunter. And when she does agree to listen, she will be impatient and laconic, giving relatively short answers to my questions. The best candidates quickly take over the conversation and dominate it. They are self-confident and relaxed. They also tend to be very articulate about their careers and themselves. The candidates I'm looking for know what they're looking for. In short, they are great interviews—if you can get them to talk to you. (Recently, a client insisted that he wanted to talk to only the candidates who refused to talk to me, the ones who weren't interested in making a move. It made my job a lot tougher, but I understood where he was coming from.)

*Be Persistent*

If there is a general motto for headhunters, this is it. If you think a particular candidate is a perfect match, do everything you can to get that person in the room with your client. For one high-profile CEO position, we were eager to get in touch with a certain U.S. senator who had just announced his retirement. Trouble was, we could never get past his chief of staff to pitch him the job. One of my partners learned that the senator was scheduled to do a book signing in Washington, D.C. She showed up at the bookstore, bought the book, and stood in line for an hour. As she handed the senator the book, she introduced herself as a headhunter and gave him a copy of the job specifications. (Watching the boss accept a blank envelope caused some distress among the senator's staffers.) She asked if they could talk about the job when he had a moment. Eventually, she and the senator had several conversations, and the once impenetrable chief of staff returned her calls—until his boss decided to run for president. His name was Bill Bradley.

### Be Patient About Discovering a Candidate's Strengths

Sixty percent of the people I interview reveal their strengths and weaknesses to me halfway through the interview. But among that other 40 percent, I have found some great managers and CEOs. I recently interviewed an extremely good candidate who pointed out that he was not the kind of guy who could walk into a roomful of strangers and soon have them all standing around, listening to him. He was not charismatic, yet he explained that his quieter style was often more effective: "I make sure that I walk up to each person, get his or her name. By the end of the evening, I've met everyone and talked to them for a bit." Some leaders are performers; others may have smaller personalities, but that does not mean they are not effective communicators.

Dull, however, is a problem. Talented people, as we have seen, have an aura about them. They are enthusiastic about their ideas and display the intensity of a master chess player. They also fill the room—something very hard to do if you are in need of a personality transplant. Dull you can spot as soon as it comes through the door. In fact, you can *hear* dullness over the phone. You can also detect someone who's performing in a way he thinks a talented interviewee ought to. Sometimes the person on the other end of the phone will begin giving a routine answer, as if he's just grabbed it off the shelf. He is not engaging in normal conversation, really telling me about himself and his goals, but *interviewing,* and thus his answers seem canned. As soon as I get off the phone, I cross him off my list. In fact, within five minutes of a pre-interview telephone conversation, I generally have a strong sense of whether this prospect is worth meeting in person.

## II. THE EFFECTIVE INTERVIEW

The key to a good job interview is digging. The good interviewer is like an archaeologist, finding one layer and then digging deeper to see what's underneath. The way headhunters confirm first impressions is by asking questions—and then asking more questions about the answers to those questions. The more you ask, the more information you will get to evaluate the person you are interviewing. To find the gems on your list of candidates, you usually have to dig deep, particularly in this competitive Talent Economy.

You have to know the right questions to ask, but above all you have to know how to listen closely and carefully. I recently heard a story about a high-level candidate who interviewed for a senior-level job at the Walt Disney Company. His interviewer talked for fifty-five minutes of the hour-long interview and then asked the candidate if he had any questions. Idiotic and useless! My best clients, in fact, do very little talking themselves. I advise letting the candidate do 80 percent of the talking. Learning how to be a skillful interviewer is about developing the right instincts. You have to learn how to identify truth—and nonsense—when you hear it. You must become skilled at listening to make sure that stories hang together and are not filled with inconsistencies. All good salespeople have surface-level answers ready to go. Anyone can repeat a story they've heard from colleagues about how a certain problem was solved. The challenge is to find out if they were actually involved in the solution. Talented people can give supporting evidence for stories about their successes and setbacks; they are able to provide the kind of details that confirm that they were really there. That is what the interview is for—to get the real story behind the top-gun résumé. Like the charming but ever crafty Detective Columbo, you enter into the relationship in a friendly, agreeable way. But you are operating out of skepticism. All your interviewees are lying murderers. Your job is to trip them up, get them to reveal the real person. In short, you must have your BS-detector turned up to high.

All your questions should try to answer these basic issues:

- How do they think?
- How do they make decisions?
- Do they have a methodology for solving problems and building organizations?
- What have they really accomplished?
- What are their leadership styles?
- Do they have the ability to overcome obstacles, to be innovative and creative?
- Do they listen to other people—particularly to customers?

### Setting the Mood

The best interviews happen when both sides are comfortable. If both people are trying to control the interview, the process can degenerate into a game where winning and losing are what count most. If the interviewer and the candidate are selling too hard, it gets difficult to break through the surface. To allow the people I'm interviewing the opportunity to shake off their nerves and prepare to be brilliant, I begin by explaining what the job is about. When I'm interviewing people for positions at my own company, I begin with some casual remarks about who we are, how our company operates, the sort of searches we specialize in. I am also willing to answer a few questions. But I avoid giving too much information about precisely what I'm looking for. If an interviewee presses me for more information, I deflect the ploy by saying something like, "We can get to that later. What I'd rather do right now is ask you some questions."

The first questions I tend to ask are also designed to make candidates feel comfortable, to keep the interview from seeming like an oral examination. We advise our headhunters to begin asking about the candidate's current job situation. My partner Steve Mader divides the interview into two parts, focusing first on questions related to what the candidate has done and knows, then moving to the issues of motivation and character. "When you begin by asking people to talk about what they do, the answers are more likely to be personal and factual," says Steve. "People tend to find it easier to talk about themselves. We are experts about ourselves; indeed our favorite subject tends to be ourselves." Right away, the interview becomes more of a friendly conversation than a test. Steve spends thirty to forty minutes on the personal stuff, and then begins to probe deeper into the place where you will find the qualities of an exceptional leader—self-knowledge. "Most people do not want to go there," Steve notes. "Managers tend to fear any situation they are not in control of. A job candidate will walk into an interview worried about how much the interviewer knows about him, what his sources are. As an interviewer, my mind is also racing: What should the right answers to my question be? What subjects should I be avoiding? These are the sorts of prejudices—on both sides—that become obstacles to good communication."

When I started out in the search business, interviews were done one-on-one, in person. In the e-world where everyone is always working and traveling, we have to pre-interview many candidates for clients via teleconferencing. Like everything else, you will get better at interviewing the more you do it. It's a good idea to tape-record your interviews (candidates usually don't mind). The first time I heard myself on tape, it was a revelation. Also: get the interview transcribed. The questions you asked—and didn't ask—will stick out more in black and white. Note especially the follow-up questions that you might have missed, and make sure you have them on hand for your next interview.

### To Get the Right Answer Requires the Right Question: My Winners

Below are some of my primary questions, and why I use them. (Christian & Timbers also has a couple of longer lists of questions for our younger associates that you may find helpful—see box, pages 131–35.)

#### "WHERE ARE YOU IN YOUR CAREER?"

It's an easy question, and it allows candidates to brag a bit about what they've done. I'm also trying to get a sense of how candidates feel about their current jobs. Generally, I like people who are happy in what they're doing. As I noted above, the best candidates are usually not looking to make a move. When people have a lot of complaints about what they are doing, I immediately wonder how long it will take before they're griping about their new job. And I definitely am not partial to managers who do a lot of blaming: "That job didn't work out because they had a lousy product." "I didn't get along with my boss." "They gave the big job to someone more senior."

Whiners are generally people who are ignorant of their own weaknesses. When things go wrong, it's always someone else's fault. Leaders are supposed to inspire their employees; they tend to be very positive people, and their enthusiasm is infectious. Negativity is also infectious, and that is a bad thing. The answer I'm looking for is an upbeat one: "I'm happy with what I'm doing. I've got an exciting job." I would follow with this question:

"WHY WOULD SOMEONE SO HAPPY WANT TO MAKE A CHANGE?"
If it is a top management job I'm interviewing for, here's the kind of answer I expect: "I want to become a CEO at some point in my career, so I think I should learn as much as possible in the process." If it is the chief executive's position I am trying to fill: "This is a chance for me to do what I've always dreamed of doing in my career—become a CEO."

Good answers. Talent is not inclined to move sideways, and no one leaves business school with the dream of rising only to general manager or even COO.

"WHAT REALLY EXCITES YOU ABOUT YOUR WORK?"
Many interviewers go through the résumé, asking about this job and that one. I'm more interested in what they like about work in general—what really makes them jump out of bed in the morning, what turns them on. Good leaders tend to say the same kinds of

things: "I love to build things. I like to get people together and attack impossible problems. Get people really excited about doing it—to figure out how to do it and get it done and then feel really good about beating the competition, getting market share." Or: "I love to see people grow in their jobs." "I love to bring people along and have their careers enhanced. I like to mentor people."

Answers like that suggest that I'm talking to a genuine leader who can inspire organizations to be successful.

### "WHAT DON'T YOU LIKE TO DO?"

Most interviewees give a pat answer: "I don't like politics." "I don't like bureaucracy." Bad answers. They don't tell me anything about your personality or those Formula Five traits. I prefer to hear such things as "I don't like marching to the beat of a drum." Or: "I hate having to do things 'the company way.' " This means you are not afraid of risk, that you are an innovator. "I don't like working with people who have personal agendas." This signals a team player.

### "WHAT WAS YOUR BEST STRATEGIC DECISION?"

Typically, a candidate will point to a major success. When I asked this question recently in an interview for the position of running global sales for a major computer maker, the candidate replied that he had turned around the business within a year. Impressive, but I was looking for the *details* on how he pulled it off—how he read the market trends, marshaled his resources, built a team for the job. That his company had increased its business was a fact. The responsibility for that success was still up for grabs unless he could give me a detailed account about how it happened. I'm also suspicious of anyone who's quick to say, "*I* turned it around . . ."

"WHY DID YOU MAKE THAT DECISION?" OR
"WHAT HAPPENED THERE?"

I am looking for good decision makers. I like to pick out various events in a career and probe them. If people have made bad decisions in their careers, they might make equally bad ones in the future. Decisions about leaving a company can be revealing. I am particularly on the lookout for answers such as, "Well, I found out later they didn't have enough money," or "I found out that they didn't have the customers they claimed they did." To me this indicates that this manager did not do his homework on the company. And if he didn't perform due diligence on a matter as important as his last job, I'm wondering what kind of rash decisions he will make in the next one.

That CFO I mentioned in the previous section has spent three years at the top of a very good company. That is a plus on his side. That the company's stock has never flown very high is a minus. Convincing Wall Street that a good company is undervalued is a major part of what a good CFO does. "What happened there?" is an obvious question. The answer will tell you a lot about whether this is the person you want to recruit for your company. Also:

### *Listen—and Probe—for Details*

Any competent businessperson will be pretty good at manipulating an interview in the direction of what he or she wants to talk about. You had better have your own bag of tricks on hand, too.

Good salespeople, for example, can recite numbers: "I increased sales volume by fifty percent, we had better closure rates than the competition, increased market share by fifteen percent and profitability by three . . ." You know the drill. My response is to take each one of those numbers and simply ask, "Well, how did you do that? What did you do there that made such a big difference?" I then listen for the details. Unless they can give me a deep description of the experience or take me through the layers of the deal, describe and enthuse about its subtleties, I know they are blowing smoke. When you have really been in battle, I mean at the front, sweating and knee-deep in gore, your war stories have an abundance of detail, energy, and authenticity not found in make-believe. I have learned to distinguish fact from fiction. Hands-on managers give you a play-by-play that confirms that they were really there.

You do not have to be an expert in every field to probe deeper. All I do is keep asking open-ended questions. "How?" "What else did you do?" "What happened then?" These all assume that there is more to say, but they are vague enough so candidates will have to think about their answers, thus giving you added insight into how their minds work.

### The Primary Pronoun Is "We"

I particularly listen for how candidates describe their relationships with their colleagues and subordinates. I am even inclined to count the number of times they say "we." The kind of manager who does not give credit to his team is the sort of person who has something to prove. As we've seen, real talent is so full of self-confidence that they have no problem sharing credit for a success. In fact, they are quick to concede that no one ever does it alone. In my experience, women are much quicker to share credit than men, too many of whom cannot seem to resist making it seem as if their organization would crumble if they did not show up for work. Honesty, as we have seen, is a crucial test of leadership, and the easiest way to see if it is valued by a manager is to listen to his tales of success. And failure.

### Inquire About Their Mistakes

I think you are likely to learn more about business leaders from how they describe their disasters than their triumphs. GE's Jack Welch has gotten a lot of mileage out of an anecdote from his first job, where he accidentally blew up a building. That he wasn't fired for this mistake, he says, convinced him of the importance of allowing people to make mistakes and learn from them. The CEO of a successful Internet company that we worked with recently asked us to find candidates who had experienced "a significant career failure." It was an unusual request—most of my clients request a shortlist of "winners"—but he explained that he himself had learned more from his setbacks than from any of his triumphs.

I always ask candidates, "Give me some examples of where you made bad decisions and tell me how you learned from those mistakes." People with high self-esteem and self-confidence know that they cannot be expected to be good at everything. Nor do they try to overcompensate for their deficiencies, like the skinny guy who likes to throw his weight around the office or the short boss who enjoys making his staff feel small.

### You Are Looking for a Builder

Talented leaders are definitely aggressive, competitive people with an inner need to win. They also like to create something out of nothing. Money is definitely important to them, but more as a scorecard. They want to make sure that they're getting the same rewards as their peers. But what they really love is to build companies, win in the marketplace, beat the competition. When Jeffrey Immelt, the man Jack Welch picked as his successor, finished business school in the early and flush 1980s, consulting firms and investment banks were waving major cash at clever young Harvard M.B.A.s like him. Unlike a lot of his classmates, Immelt passed. "I always wanted to build things and to lead groups of people," recalled the new CEO. GE offered him that opportunity and he signed on. Smart move—on both sides, it turns out.

You want to hear job candidates echo Immelt. You also want them to give you plenty of examples of the kinds of teams they've built. When someone says, "I love to build teams," press them with: "So, tell me about a team that you built and how you built it." Get them to define what they mean by "team." (And don't forget to listen for how many times they say "I" instead of "we.")

### Be on the Lookout for Signals

You have to read between the lines. When candidates offer such "mistakes" as "Well, I shouldn't have taken that job," or "I should have left that company earlier," they're not really describing something that went wrong. And when you rephrase the question—"I meant a bad decision, a strategic mistake"—and they don't deliver, you've got to ask yourself, "Do I believe this guy?" Listening to the candidate is crucial; so is taking good notes. But equally important is paying attention to your gut.

I have tried to train myself to hear how people think. You, too, can do it. The key is to listen hard, focusing not just on the words but also on how genuinely and enthusiastically they are delivered.

Good actors have to work hard at playing enthusiasm. You can learn to spot a phony a mile away.

### Pay Attention to Body Language

Exceptional leaders are decisive; they get to the point. That's usually because they've already thought through every angle. The best leaders have already raised every possible question in their own mind (and answered them) before they sit down to discuss a problem. So if you ask a question and the candidate hesitates, it probably means something. When the issue of why a candidate is willing to make a move comes up, Steve Mader focuses on body language. "I watch how fast the response comes," he says. "If someone takes time to ponder the direction of her career, there are two possible answers why: (1) she is actually quite satisfied with her current position; or (2) she doesn't really know what to say because she has not given the possibility of taking another job much thought." The candidate who has thought carefully about making a change will answer articulately and persuasively. "If a person seems to be thinking it through on the spot, you will probably be able to tell," explains Steve. We are looking for the candidate who is comfortable with questions and ready with a concise answer.

### Pay Attention to the Questions They Ask

Talented people are likely to ask a lot of questions that are not only incisive but reveal much about how their minds work, how strategically they think, how creative they are. As we saw in chapter two, great business leaders have a way of talking about their work; there is a formula, a methodology, that they use over and over. You have to be listening for an echo of that formula in what your candidates are saying. In every interview you do, the same question must hover in the air: "Is this person the absolute best I can get for this job at this time?"

### Selling Is a Two-way Street

You are doing the interviewing, but in most cases you will also be selling your company and yourself. Most employers want the candidate to show up wanting the job. My best clients, however, are usually interested in people who don't want the job. Typically, when you call a candidate cold and request an interview, the best candidates will say, "Well, let me think about it. I'm not certain I want to take the next step."

That's when you begin to sell them. You have got to make every job candidate see themselves in the future—theirs and yours. Most of the people you will be talking to will be calculating your interest against their momentum in their current position. If they're on an upward trajectory, they are going to be that much less interested in an alternative. In other words, they are looking at things in the exact opposite way you are: you want them to think of the future; they can only think of the present and the past. Your challenge as an employer—who has learned to think like a headhunter—is to help this manager see what your company will look like a year from now. *With him in a top position.* You have to impress upon him that the company he will be joining will be different from the company as it is. *Because of his very presence.* It will be a better company, a more successful company. That's why you want him.

Your hardest job will be to excite his imagination with the fabulous prospects that lay ahead by virtue of his talent, his leadership.

In my opinion, selling the candidate on the job is half of the interview, maybe even two-thirds. Because once they say, "Okay, I'll talk to you," then you've got them interested. If they're as good as you think they are, they'll do their homework on the company that's recruiting them and decide, "Hey, this is interesting." Why have they shown up for the interview? They were flattered, they are curious, they're looking to be sold. To sell them, you have to capture their imaginations. The best talent, as I have stressed, likes to think strategically. Therefore, you increase your odds of luring that kind of person by getting her to think strategically about your company with her in it. I guarantee that if you pose the possibilities in that way, you will immediately feel the candidate's excitement. Talent is turned on by challenge, and by infusing their imaginations with the prospects of challenges and opportunities—namely, joining your team—you will have pushed the right button.

### Get a Second Opinion

I advise my clients to get as deeply involved in the interview process as possible. In most cases, you will know whether a particular candidate is the person for you. Some candidates deliver quickly on all the objective measures in an interview. The Formula Five is there, and they have a good answer for every question. Recently, I interviewed someone for a top job, and she was brilliant answering my questions. She positively nailed the interview, almost before I could get a take on her personally. Almost. There was a red flag. She was so good at answering the questions that she came off as a bit arrogant. I was concerned that maybe this candidate was too concerned that things get done her way. But she was so good on every other measure that I was unwilling to trust my own intuition. I advised my client that this candidate was extremely impressive and said all the right things, as far as I was concerned, but I wanted him to talk to her, and then we'd talk. He, too, found her too single-minded. The company needed more of a team player, and he passed.

If you have any doubts, get someone else to talk to the candidate. Even with all my experience interviewing managers, I often find it very useful to compare notes with two people who've recently talked to the candidate. I also don't have a problem after an interview calling around for some more feedback on a candidate, especially now that I've met the person and have my own take. If the job is important to you, then it's worth the time to satisfy any doubts you may have.

### Warning: You Have Created a Monster

You have been trying to persuade a person who was not looking for a job to consider the possibilities of making a change. Now that you've got him on the hook, he will then decide—because he's the smart, analytical, and strategic manager you've been looking for— to take the next four calls that come in from headhunters. "If I'm going to take another job," his reasoning will go, "I might as well check out all the opportunities available."

And suddenly you are in a competitive environment. Worse still, you might just lose. How can that be? Several reasons: you haven't taken the time to get to know the candidate or let him get to know you. You haven't given him the opportunity to connect with other people in your company so that he already has the "feel" of that team. Then there's the chance that he'll be talking to some of your customers to find out how great they think you are. Clearly, you've still got some hard work to do.

### Headhunting Is a Lot Like Dating

As you might have noticed. And just like in dating, while you have to be prepared for rejection, persistence does pay off. The best candidates are worth romancing. One client we did a search for invited a candidate to town with his wife and set them up for the weekend at a great hotel, bottle of wine and flowers in the room, tickets to a popular show. All those little touches showed how much they wanted this person. Simply by placing a call, you have expressed your interest. The next step is to get them to hug you back.

### Making the Emotional Connection

Interviews are useful for both sides to size each other up. But remember, you are trying to fire up their imaginations to the point where they begin seeing themselves as a member of your team. There is no better substitute for that than giving them a taste of what playing your game is really like. Here's a list of my favorite strategies for helping a candidate see his name on one of your company's business cards. Invite them:

- to join you on a couple of sales calls to your prime customers
- to sit in on a strategy meeting with the company's top management
- to meet with your investment bankers to hear what they're saying

to investors about the IPO (or secondary public offering)

- to meet with members of your board (if it's a position in top management)
- to bring their significant other to dinner with you and yours
- to go for a long walk and talk about careers and life, your past and her future
- to play a couple of rounds of golf at a great course. (Friends who golf tell me that they would consider trading their firstborn, never mind their job, for a free weekend playing a world-class course like Pebble Beach or Shinnecock Hills; if the candidate likes fishing or sailing or roulette, act accordingly.)

The possibilities are limited only by your own imagination. The goal is to create a situation where some major bonding can take place. You are asking this extremely talented person to jettison all alternatives for you. The response you're looking for is: "Hey, I like this person. I want to work with him."

### My Puzzlers

I want to get a sense of how a candidate's mind works, how he or she thinks. Sometimes I lay out a difficult, virtually impossible, situation and ask them how they'd handle it. My goal is to watch them think it through and see how fast they come up with a reasonable answer. Everyone in business has been up against a major conundrum, either a problem you've solved or one where you've made a big mistake. By now you know the answer. Throw it out on the table to see how the new person might handle it.

For example: you're the new CEO, you're about to end your first quarter on the job, and you are absurdly late in your product shipments because you've had delays in bringing a new product on line. You have old product in inventory, but you've refrained from selling or shipping it because you promised—you sold your customers—the new product. But you don't have it; indeed, you have just learned that the new stuff will not be ready for another three or four months. The horrifying result is that at the end of your first quarter in the top job, you have sold nothing and therefore will definitely not make your quarter projections. It's a disaster. Your customers will be outraged, the word will get out, and your stock will plummet. You might lose your job.

What should you do? . . . Time's up. The right answer is that you figure out how to sell the *old* product. You do whatever it takes. You're going to go out and meet with all your customers personally; indeed, all your people are going to head into the field and talk to your customers. You're going to get them to work with you. You go to your customers and say, "I'll tell you what. I'm going to sell you the old product for a much cheaper price, and it's going to work for you. And you know what else I'm going to do? We'll give you an automatic upgrade with the new product as soon it's deliverable. You've got to work with me on this."

Try it out the next time you interview someone for a job.

### My Favorite Trick Questions

I like to pick out a few things in a candidate's career and burrow into them. Sometimes the best way to get candidates to reveal their deeper selves or to get past their defenses is to trick them into honesty.

"WHAT IS THE PROUDEST MOMENT OF YOUR CAREER?"
Most people cite an accomplishment. In a recent interview with a candidate who was running an $800 million division of a major tech company, I asked him what his biggest strategic success was. "Turning around the consumer business in eighteen months," he said proudly. I cared less about the achievement than how he did it (or if he did it all by himself, which is usually doubtful). But once I have him on the subject, I can ask more about it, delve deeper into the details. All it takes is to keep asking "How?" "Why did you do that?" "How did you make that happen?" "How did you come to that conclusion?" "When did you make that decision?"

This candidate answered each question with plenty of details. It was clear that this business turnaround had so consumed him for a year and a half that he could have written a book about what happened. That is what you want.

"WHAT DO YOU THINK YOUR STRENGTHS ARE?"
A main objective in every interview I do is to identify core skills. Few candidates can resist boasting about their triumphs, and if all their wins are in an expertise different from the one they're being interviewed for, I've learned something important (while giving the candidate the opportunity to brag about past exploits).

"WHAT DO YOU THINK ARE THE MISCONCEPTIONS ABOUT YOU?"
This is a particular favorite of mine, and I rarely resist asking it. Most people assume that I'm looking for them to be critical of themselves, so they try to be candid (though not too candid): "People will say I'm too tough." "People will say I'm not tough enough." A few with a keen sense of language get the trick right away: a mis-

conception, by definition, is a mistaken interpretation, a misunderstanding, and therefore will not be correct. But the answers that people give can be very revealing about how they view themselves, not to mention their sense of how others view them.

### *The Biggest Obstacles to Becoming a Good Interviewer*

NOT DOING YOUR HOMEWORK

For anyone who is new to job interviewing—and even professional headhunters have to start somewhere—your toughest task is understanding precisely what a specific job entails. What are the responsibilities of a chief financial officer? No matter how bright or ambitious one of our young recruiters might be, at twenty-six, he might not have a clue that a CFO, while acting as company comptroller, is also the company treasurer, who does financial analysis, supervises the company's tax liabilities, *and* manages relations with shareholders and investors. Of course, most CEOs and top managers know what a CFO does. But even experienced hiring managers will have gaps in their knowledge. Consider the CEO with a technical background who has to hire a top sales or marketing executive to take his growing company to the next level. Now that he's created a new, exciting product, he will have to educate himself in the nuances of product management and distribution to find the right person for the job.

I also expect CEOs or selection committees to be a bit fuzzy about exactly what some of their managers in the forefront of computer and Internet technology do. Even headhunters have to work hard to keep up. "Chief information officer" has become an increasingly important post, but many top executives in traditional companies may not yet realize that keeping up with advances in e-commerce and information technology may require a major new management position. For headhunters, familiarity with the contents of every job description comes with years of experience meeting with clients and job candidates, talking with consultants, figuring out how various industries work. But if you want the most talented people in those jobs, you better know the specifics and nuances of the jobs you're hiring for. It is bound to make you a better interviewer. To ask the right questions of any job candidate, you have to know a great deal about the job you're trying to fill.

How to get up to speed? Do the reporting: (a) call your friends who understand the specialty; (b) call someone who's an expert who is not a friend; (c) learn from the people that you talk to in the interview process. This, of course, can prove to be a worst-case scenario, because you're flying blind, without preparation. Yet often you can learn as much about the job description as you can about the interviewee by picking his brain. As headhunters, we are not always experts on the particular industry or business a client is in. It is amazing, however, how much we learn throughout the interviewing process about the nature of the work involved in a particular position for a particular client operating in a particular market. Even if you think you know enough about what a general manager of sales or a production manager does, by talking to as many experts as possible you will become a much better-informed interviewer.

## NOT GETTING BEYOND THE RÉSUMÉ

The easiest way to do an interview is to do it according to the candidate's résumé. He had that job, then he went there, and there, and now he's here. "What did you do in that job?" "Why did you leave?" And so on. Those are decent enough questions, but you will get better answers by doing some research on the companies the candidate has worked for, or by educating yourself a bit about the industry, if it is different from yours. Often the business or corporate environment a person works in will color our assessment of her achievements and ambition. Equally often we will be wrong on all counts because we do not have the slightest clue as to what has been happening in that industry or company. For example: according to the résumé, the candidate has worked seven years for a company that has not performed well in an industry of no winners, the rental car business. Why did she stay in that job? It's an extremely good question, and the answer might be one you would like. Some people need to win so badly that they couldn't work for a company that was not a leader in its field or shaking up the marketplace. If you're one of those people, then your first impression of the candidate will be that she doesn't seem like the strongest player in the game.

But not everyone can work for a major winner, and certain industries have their ups and downs. Also, some very good managers do not evaluate themselves only on the scale of winning and losing. Their measure might be, "Am I meeting other people's expectations? Am I getting the job done?" Or an executive might have made a valiant attempt to turn the company into a winner. That is why she was promoted four times in seven years. It is also why she is finally willing to consider a move: she's giving up, conceding— "I'm too good to keep killing myself, trying to turn a loser into a winner. It's time to move on." You won't see any of that unless you do more than just peruse her résumé.

Recruiting is a world of illusion. A candidate walks through the door and is a big question mark. It makes the task of filling a job a lot easier if there is an objective measure—evidence that she's done the job before, preferably at a reputable company, that she's been to the right college, the best B-school, and so on. Harvard Business School and General Electric thought this person was smart and talented. The hard fact is that none of that is proof that a person can really do the job, because the job you're trying to fill will have its own responsibilities and challenges unique to your company and the subtleties and complexities of your business at a certain moment in time. You have to figure out how this candidate will fit into your needs, and that will take some work on your part as you discover what those needs really are and who this candidate really is. Headhunters learn very early in their careers that candidates who look good or bad on the face of it will often look quite different when you do some digging and begin asking the right questions.

NOT KNOWING WHAT YOU'RE LOOKING FOR

One of the important messages in the Talent Economy is that no company, industry, or CEO has a death grip on talent. Who is your choice? The manager working for a great company who is not going anywhere? Or the guy from an also-ran operation who is brilliant, motivated, and an impressive strategic thinker? The latter is obviously your candidate, and, just as obviously, you're going to have to work very hard to find him.

What you see is not always what you get. How about someone who just got fired? At first blush, that is a negative. But if you make an effort to find out the real story why he got the sack—his boss was threatened by his talent and vision and squeezed him out—he may be the person you're looking for. (Henry Ford II fired Lee Iacocca, who went on to do just fine running Chrysler.) How often do CEOs bring in an heir apparent and then sabotage him? The inability of strong leaders to admit that there is anyone out there talented enough to replace them is a staple of business school case studies. Picking up a world-class manager who's just been pushed from a corner office could be a wonderful opportunity.

Professional interviewers soon learn that evaluating executives is a relative and situational undertaking. The good news is that you can find all sorts of gems in struggling companies. Moreover, how attractive your company is to an outsider is equally relative. You might think you are struggling more than ever, while from the standpoint of someone from another company that is in real trouble, your company might appear to be the perfect opportunity. In a competitive Talent Economy, you will have to find talent in unexpected places.

But your job is not over once you hire exceptional people. Your next challenge is to hold on to your talent.

---

## The Questions You Need to Ask

At Christian & Timbers, each consultant and associate uses a variety of interviewing questions and techniques to develop a thorough understanding of a candidate. The list below summarizes several questions we developed specifically for interviewing a CEO-level candidate to gain insight into his or her personal experiences and qualities. As you use these questions, look for responses that highlight how the individual has behaved in previous circumstances. Past behavior is the best predictor of future behavior, and, as the interviewer, you want to know how the candidate will act to meet challenges within your own organization.

1. How political or bureaucratic is your current organization, and how do you solve problems in this environment? What actions do you take?

2. How do you communicate a vision to a large group of people and keep them focused on execution? What techniques do you use?

3. How do you build or change the image of a company?

4. What do you think about in your job? Where do you spend your time?

5. What have been your most critical decisions, and what was your thought process behind them? What information did you look for? What did you do that didn't work?

6. When you move into a new job, how do you evaluate your key people and decide how to build your team?

7. What was your biggest surprise in your first general manager's role? How did you handle the situation?

8. Compare your past two roles. What was different about each? What did you do differently as a result of these different situations? How would you translate this experience into future assignments?

9. What kind of interactions have you had with the board of directors?

10. How do you approach your start in a new role? What do you look for? What actions do you take?

11. Good CEOs develop their team effectively. How do

    you develop people into larger roles? How do you mentor your staff?

12. Who is the best person that ever worked for you? Why do you feel this way about him or her?

13. When you find bright people in your organization, how do you keep them motivated and committed to the company?

The following is a list we usually refer to in our firm as the "tough questions." Here you're looking to get deeper into the candidate's self-knowledge, that second phase of the interview that, as Steve Mader pointed out, is the real challenge. With excellent setup of the specific company situation, these questions also develop insight into a candidate's capabilities. As you use these questions, look for responses that highlight how the individual has behaved in previous circumstances. Again, past behavior is the best predictor of future behavior.

1. What is your management style and how would you rate yourself as a manager?

2. How would you describe your personality?

3. What do you look for when you hire people?

4. Have you ever had to fire people? What were the reasons and how did you handle the situation?

5. What do you think is the most difficult aspect of being a manager?

6. In your current position, what features do you like the most? The least?

7. What were your most significant accomplishments in your last position? In your career?
8. Give me an example of a serious conflict you had with someone and how you resolved it.
9. What are the important trends or cutting-edge issues in your industry?
10. What qualities or skills make a good manager?
11. What do you think of your former boss?
12. Describe a situation in which your work was criticized.
13. Tell me about one of your failures and how you handled it.
14. What are your strong points?
15. What are your weaknesses?
16. What would your boss say if I asked him/her about your strengths and weaknesses?
17. What misconceptions do others have about you?
18. Where do you see yourself in five years?
19. If you could start your career over again, what would you do differently?
20. How would you define success, and how successful do you feel you've been so far in your career?
21. How do you stay current with what is going on in the marketplace (new technologies, etc.)?
22. Describe a difficult decision you had to make. What were the results of the decision?
23. If you were to make a move, what would it take (in terms of compensation or responsibility)?
24. Tell me about a time you were faced with a difficult ethical dilemma and how you dealt with it.

25. How long will it take you to make a meaningful contribution to our organization?
26. Give me an example of how you provided leadership and direction under unusually difficult circumstances.
27. Give me an example of how you helped a subordinate develop personal and professional skills? Where else do you think you could have helped this individual? If you were to improve this person's skills as an executive in just one important way to make them more effective, what would that be?
28. What do you expect out of this position and your association with our company?
29. What would be the first thing you'd do in this new job? What would you change about this company?

## CHAPTER 5

## *Who Would Leave a Company Like This?*

In a Talent Economy, the best managers can choose from a long list of impressive jobs with the biggest brands in the nation, and more people than ever are making the big move. The executive turnover rate is between 10 and 17 percent, an eighteen-year high. But it has become increasingly difficult for many less glamorous companies to recruit the kind of exceptionally talented people they will need to continue prospering. There is, however, a simple alternative: keep the talent you have. Your challenge is to prove to your best people that staying put is the smartest move of their careers.

It will also save you a lot of money. Ernst & Young, the $5 billion accounting and consulting firm, estimates that it costs them 150 percent of an annual salary to replace an employee, including the costs of training a new person and the problems it causes in the department and among clients. In fact, most companies are now estimating that replacing talent will cost up to three times the salary of the person lost. As a headhunter, I spend most of my time trying to persuade talent to jump ship. Every time a top prospect turns me down flat, I want to know why. Over the years, I have analyzed how the best companies keep their talent. Low turnover is no accident. Today's talent-smart companies such as E&Y, General Electric, Cisco, Southwest Airlines, and Goldman Sachs have devised a wide array of strategies to keep their best employees from resigning. Retention starts before recruitment. When people are considering a new job, they want to know what the company is like, whom they'll be working with and for, what the work arrangements are, and how the company recognizes achievement. While some people will jump for just the money, most talented people are looking for a much bigger package. To become what I like to call "the employer of choice," you have to create a culture centered around keeping your employees happy and motivated.

### Why People Leave

Contrary to popular opinion, employee loyalty is not a thing of the past. Current figures from the Bureau of Labor Statistics indicate that the share of American workers with at least ten years working for the same company has remained at about 30 percent since 1983. Even today's men and women in the twenty-five-to-thirty-four-year age range are sticking in there at pretty much the same rates. According to a recent survey by Fortune Personnel Consultants, more than 90 percent of the employees they surveyed said that they felt "very loyal" or "somewhat loyal" to their companies.

Apparently, companies have to work pretty hard to lose people's loyalty. In my experience, here are the reasons people typically give for quitting:

- boredom or lack of challenging work
- limited opportunities for growth or advancement
- unreasonable work hours
- no leeway for balancing work and family
- lack of appreciation from superiors
- a hypercritical boss
- a boss running on a personal agenda
- manipulative or selfish superiors
- lack of leadership or poor supervision
- no mentoring
- no clear career paths
- low expectations and standards for the job
- too many conflicts and in-fighting with petty colleagues or bosses
- too many repetitive problems
- too much bureaucracy
- inferior or ineffective coworkers
- others stealing your ideas without giving you credit
- the company refuses to listen to customers
- they put the wrong person in a job for the wrong reasons—above you
- the company is not willing to embrace change
- the company is not a winner
- noncompetitive compensation packages
- long commute
- because something has occurred that is "the last straw"

Most of the above causes can be chalked up to bad leadership, although in some cases it is sour grapes. But when complaints become widespread in any company, it's time to reevaluate. When the air is filled with whining and recriminations, when managers are spending more time fighting one another than the competition, real talent is going to have an eye on the door.

Here's what talent-smart companies do to increase the odds of keeping their best people:

### *The Winningest Strategy Is—Winning*

The one common denominator I see as a headhunter in job candidates, top managers, boards, and even venture capitalists is that they all want to be part of an exclusive club. Who doesn't want to be a winner? You have an edge over the competition, major resources to get the job done, plenty of money to go around. It's easier, and it's fun. A successful company peopled with talent will feed off itself. Build a successful company and talent will not only come, it will stay.

No company has been at the top of everyone's list of great American companies longer than General Electric. Twenty years ago, GE's market value was a bit more than $12 billion; today it's worth *$500 billion.* The reason, as everyone knows, is Jack Welch. Even his enemies admire and envy him. Welch has retired, and in just about any other company, losing such a living legend would be a matter for concern. But GE's real secret sauce is people. As we have seen, a great leader is a powerful magnet for talent, and the bench at GE is deep with terrific managerial talent. Any company would be delighted to have any manager from GE. If you could even get them on the phone to make an offer. Over the years, several of Welch's direct reports left, mainly because they were relatively young executives who knew they would have to wait a decade or longer for the chance to succeed Welch. Instead, they went off to run their own operations, and brilliantly. Larry Bossidy, who retired in 2000 from a successful stint running Allied Signal; Intuit's Stephen Bennett; Thomas Rogers, who runs Primedia; SPX chief John Blystone; Polaris Industry CEO Thomas Tiller; Conseco's Gary Wendt—they're all Welch protégés. Two of the finalists-in-waiting for Welch's job went off to run 3M and Home Depot within days of Welch's announcement that their colleague Jeffrey Immelt, the forty-four-year-old head of GE Medical Systems, would be his successor. It's an amazing list. But many other formidable talents have happily stayed on. Leaving a company as good as GE is likely to feel like taking a step down, and it is hardly surprising that headhunters rate GE as the hardest company to recruit talent from.

In fact, other corporations have equally impressive (or even better) retention rates, and upon examination, such superstar corporations as GE, Southwest Airlines, Cisco, Home Depot, and Goldman Sachs are often rated not simply as great companies but also as great places to work. If you compare the perennials on *Fortune*'s list of the nation's "Most Admired Companies" with the magazine's list of the "Best Companies to Work For," you will find much overlap. Success seems to be a mutual admiration society with talent at its center: to become successful, you need talent; to remain successful, you need to keep your talent. And to assure a low turnover rate, you will have to keep your people happy. Here are what talent-smart companies do to keep the circle of talent spinning:

### The Quickest Defensive Tactic: Money

And every variation thereof, mainly in creatively devised stock options. Over the years, I have found that a major reason why people are not eager to leave their current employer is because they are holding millions of dollars in unvested stock options. GE, for example, is notorious for making sure that a large chunk of the stock options they award their best performers vest only at retirement. You don't stay, you don't get the money. (An astonishing figure just came across my desk: a decade ago, CEOs of the nation's 200 largest companies were paid an average of $2.8 million a year; by 1999 the number had more than tripled, to $9.4 million, fueled mainly by stock options that had accounted for more than half of the pay packages.) In the past few years, law firms have been forced to compete for talent by raising associates' salaries by as much as 50 percent. A new recruit at a big New York City firm now starts at upwards of $175,000. To hold on to their talent, consulting partnerships, which are not public companies and therefore have no stock to offer employees, formed investment funds in new companies so that they could share some of that wealth with young associates. To respond to the Internet speed of potential offers, many old-economy companies are juicing up their employment practices. Disney and FedEx, for instance, have given certain executives the authority to raise salaries on the spot.

In the war for talent, you cannot be stingy. If you do not compensate your best people well enough, someone else will. I advise companies to review their compensation packages regularly and to make sure they are not falling behind the competition. If you are confused about what you should be paying, hire a search firm to do a "competitive compensation analysis" to determine what the appropriate compensation package for each executive position ought to be. Believe me, if you do not know what the market will bear, your talent will. Sure, you expect your home-run hitters to hit home runs. But if they break records and make your company a lot of money, then maybe you should redistribute some of that wealth in annual bonuses, competency-based pay, profit sharing, and tuition reimbursement. Happy, well-paid employees are inclined to stay put. I know, because they refuse to take my calls.

### Recognition

Who doesn't like a pat on the back? Most good companies compensate their top people adequately. Often, though, they forget to reaffirm their appreciation of a job well done by actually saying it. Talent wants respect and recognition, and the best companies make an effort to be generous with their praise, too. They also promote their best people quickly and often. "You want a place that rewards you for contributing by giving you opportunity, not a place that does everything by seniority," advises Charles R. Lee, the chairman and co-chief executive of Verizon Communications.

### More Responsibility and Autonomy

Becoming a CEO is what talent has been dreaming about since day one. Give your top people something to run before someone else does. Push decision making as far down into the organization as you can. If you're a big company, you have divisions and departments to hand out. General Electric's stars get to run company operations such as GE Financial Services, GE Medical Services, GE Appliances, GE Lighting, GE Capital, GE Asia-Pacific, not to mention NBC—divisions of General Electric that are bigger than most independent companies. There are business reasons for such divisions, but there are also talent reasons. Microsoft has literally hundreds of general managers in charge of their various products. Tell me that it doesn't help retain people when they are able to say, "I'm a GM at Microsoft."

The companies that have the lowest turnover rates tend to embrace new ideas. Strong companies like GE, IBM, Hewlett-Packard, and 3M are quick to allow their best people to take their great ideas and start new divisions or even new businesses. Hewlett-Packard created Agilent; 3Com launched Palm.

### *Be an Environmentalist*

I'm not talking tree-hugger here (though I'm all for trees). I'm talking about creating the kind of supportive and challenging workplace that makes it hard for people to leave. If you're the kind of boss who likes yes-men, then you cannot expect innovative people or brilliant mavericks to stick around and wait while you scream at them. If you're a stickler for numbers and ducks in a row, talented people who believe there is more to business than spreadsheets will not want to stay. Use your head, definitely; but have a heart, too, and you will be amazed by the dividends that this kind of compassionate capitalism can deliver in employee loyalty and retention rates.

### *Do the Right Thing—Even if It Threatens the Bottom Line*

Several years ago a talented headhunter joined the Boston office of Christian & Timbers. At the end of his first year with us, his thirty-five-year-old brother, who had been fighting lymphoma, began to fail. He wanted to spend time with him in New York, but he was involved in several major searches in the Boston area and was concerned about not delivering for his clients. It was a difficult dilemma for the company—but not *that* difficult. Clearly he had to spend time with his dying brother. We cut him loose, and he spent the next four and a half months with his brother. After his brother died, he returned to the office and discovered to his amazement that he had been one of the company's most successful performers! His three colleagues in the Boston office had not only conducted his interviews, made the client presentations, and closed his searches, but they had also initiated new searches—and gave him credit for everything.

Needless to say, he was grateful. But so were we. As we said to him at the time, "You showed us how to be a brother."

### Encourage the Innovators and Entrepreneurs in Your Company

And then point out the advantage of being a risk taker inside an established, stable organization. It is called "corporate venturing" and "intrapreneurship"—creating entrepreneurial businesses inside larger corporations. Bell Atlantic, Texas Instruments, 3M, IBM, Dupont, and Wal-Mart, among others, have successfully set up formal programs to encourage in-house entrepreneurs. As much as talented people will be drawn to start-ups, they are not unaware of the risks. If you offer them the challenges of being out there on the edge with no abyss to step into, they are more likely to stick with you—and create additional value for your company with their ideas. Check out the successful companies you admire, and you will find a work environment that breeds innovation.

*Create a Culture of Learning and Mentoring*

Talented people are smart enough to know that they need experience and coaching. If you make it clear that your organization is the kind of place where leaders are cultivated, that your company is a kind of launching pad for executive stars, young hotshots will line up outside your door. The number of famous CEOs who came out of consulting firms like McKinsey and Booz-Allen is astonishing, and it is no surprise that, over the years, those firms have had their pick of young talent.

To encourage your employees to take their work to the next level, help them envision new goals. Make it company policy for top management to mentor those under them, advising them at every stage of their careers. "How do you really feel about your job?" "Are you having fun, or is it a drag?" "Do you think you're moving at the pace you anticipated, or do you think you should be moving faster?" "Where do you want to go next?" "How can I help you get there?" "How am I doing as a mentor?" Smart companies get their top people involved early with their talented young up-and-comers. At Deloitte & Touche Consulting, one of *Fortune*'s "Best Companies to Work For," senior partners are assigned as mentors to the firm's most promising younger partners.

Make sure people are learning, getting better, creating a career path that keeps moving upward. Compensate good performance. Invest real money in their training and move the best people up as soon as possible. In a company as huge as GE, Jack Welch was not able to be everyone's mentor. But every spring he spent a week with his HR chief, evaluating the company's talent. GE managers prepare "résumés" of their accomplishments, strengths, and wish lists for promotions, which they discuss with *their* managers, who then recommend the best candidates to Welch. He and his head of personnel then select 360 for GE's celebrated management training program, which is taught by key GE executives. GE also has another program for managers, held four times a year, where they work on some of the tougher problems the company is up against. Such internal training programs are a win-win situation for all concerned: young managers know that their bosses are paying attention, and the top execs can watch their rising stars in action. Develop your reputation as a leader-producing machine, and talent will want to be part of your mission.

### Make Sure Your Managers Are Visible and Accessible

It is amazing how much goodwill you can get out of periodic visits to the shop floor or to the company's outposts to chat up the troops and pat some backs. The first thing one turnaround specialist I know does when he arrives at a troubled company is take a can of paint into the parking lot and paint out the names of top managers on reserved parking spots. He wants to give his top executives the opportunity to walk through the parking lot and talk to their employees. He has also made a point of always lunching in the company cafeteria and routinely donning a hard hat to visit the shop floor. How will employees know their bosses really care if they never see them? Let them know it is okay to ask questions. Find out what they want, what they think is missing. Create an open environment where people aren't afraid to talk to one another.

*Cultivate Your Geeks and Techies*

Traditionally, they have been the people who have worked in obscurity. But the nerds have inherited the earth (at least the marketplace part of it). The people who know the technology and keep up with it are the only ones standing between you and some very unhappy customers. Try to understand what it is they do, and make sure they're comfortable telling you the truth. Let them know that their opinions matter and that they are key to the company's success. Brilliant engineers and technicians are often immune to promotion into high-level management jobs, preferring a niche where they can keep dreaming up and designing new products. In recent years, IBM, Cisco, Xerox, Sun Microsystems, and Microsoft have devised variations of what Microsoft has called its "distinguished engineer" awards, a kind of Silicon Valley version of the Nobel Prize. Every year, for example, Microsoft rewards four or five talented engineers with a financial package equivalent to that of a Microsoft vice president.

*Embrace Diversity*

There is a generational change happening out there. Today's teenagers and twenty-somethings are very comfortable with diversity and different lifestyles. Studies are beginning to show that creative young workers are more attracted to companies that are visibly comfortable with women, people of color, and homosexuals. So if you were worried about that brilliant kid with the tattoos and pierced eyebrow scaring away your customers, be aware that she might be just the ticket for attracting more talent to your organization.

*Encourage a Balance Between Work and Life*

If you believe the press, the stereotype that the Internet pioneers are most proud of is "workaholic." You may not have to set up bunk beds in the office, but hard work and boundless energy are, as we have seen, the mark of great leadership. But if you cannot afford to counter every offer with bigger bucks, you might try creating a workplace that is a little more family-friendly. We all want to wake up in the morning eager to go to work. For some, all that takes is dollar signs, or more responsibility, or more power. For others, it's working for a company that recognizes that there are other things in life besides the marketplace. Workplace studies indicate that today's executives want more time with their families. Several years ago, Ernst & Young, for example, discovered that 20 percent of their men and women in top management were leaving annually, and more than half of those folks were quitting because the hours were destroying their family life. CEO Philip Laskawy immediately recognized that the cost of losing (and replacing) such talent was huge—not to mention the price of losing continuity with important customers. E&Y's 600-employee San Jose office, in the heart of Silicon Valley, was hemorrhaging talent to nearby tech companies. By 1997, half the San Jose office's professional staff had been with Ernst & Young for less than two years. Recognizing that E&Y would have to reshape the way it did business, Laskawy established an "Office of Rentention"—the first in the nation— devoted to figuring out how the company could still focus on the customers who were crucial to its survival without burning out its best people. Laskawy then made it very clear to the company that the head of the Office of Retention would be reporting directly to him. Four years later, E&Y had managed to knock several points off its turnover rates for men and women. The company remains committed to providing a work-life balance for all its 34,000 professionals—starting with CEO Laskawy and the firm's partners, who have given their subordinates (and themselves) the freedom not to check phone messages and e-mails over weekends and have put a cap on billable hours. The company has even set up "workload patrols" to review time sheets to make sure people aren't overwhelmed. E&Y has also shifted travel schedules so that its people don't have to spend so many days on the road (and so many weekends recovering).

Employees still work very hard at E&Y, and Laskawy is still not satisfied with his solutions. But the company is impressing not only its current employees but future prospects whose ambitions also include happy marriages, children's birthdays, and school events. To prove its long-term commitment to balancing work and life at Ernst & Young, the company promoted the head of its Office of Retention to partner.

### *Put an Executive in Charge of Protecting Your Environment*

To prevent larger problems down the line, you have to have someone ready to handle the piddling stuff. All of us who have worked in large organizations know how small problems can turn into issues people end up quitting over. One manager who steals someone's ideas or another who likes to make his people work late can stir up resentment. As demands on time in the workplace increase, as stress builds, someone has to be paying attention and be able to defuse the situation quickly. Of course you care about your employees. But top management is busy and stressed, too. Follow E&Y's lead and make it someone's job to care for the employee-first environment that is crucial to keeping the best people from signing on with the competition.

### Small Things Can Add Up to Big Dividends

Studies show that little perks can boost employee morale. Health- and dental-care programs and educational opportunities or tuition reimbursements can prove that management is serious about taking care of its employees. Offering casual dress codes, on-site massages, and employee gyms can help reduce stress and overwork, not to mention medical problems that increase company insurance costs. Anything that can keep people productive while allowing them to juggle their home and family commitments is usually appreciated. Valet dry cleaning services and car washes are also appearing on corporate premises all over the nation. Employees appreciate the convenience, and their bosses don't have to worry about people sneaking off the reservation to get their errands done. Many companies now offer daycare programs for kids—a big plus in retaining top female executives. Cisco recently completed a state-of-the-art daycare center with a video monitoring system that allows parents to check on their kids from various areas throughout the Cisco complex.

### Foster a Sense of Community with Your Community

Many companies these days have "mission statements" that assert the company's commitment to its customers, the community, even the environment. Some of those companies actually *live* their values, not only encouraging their employees to volunteer for community groups, but giving them the opportunity to do it on company time. Tom Chappell, the cofounder and CEO of Tom's of Maine, the company that invented natural toothpaste and has pioneered "values oriented" capitalism, not only reserves 10 percent of his company's profits for charitable giving, but for over a decade he has been encouraging employees to spend 5 percent of the company's time on volunteer work. Periodically, the whole company will spend a day working on a community project such as cleaning up a local river.

Such community outreach is no longer limited to small companies. Valero Energy, an $8 billion utility company based in San Antonio, also has a mission statement encouraging employees to become community leaders and donate 1 percent of their income to United Way's Care Share program (for every dollar donated, Valero adds another fifty cents); most employees also spend two hours a month with the company's Volunteer Council, which works with local charities. When floods hit Texas in the summer of 1999, the company gave $5,000 each to three employees who were flooded out, and the Volunteer Council worked with other groups to clean up the mess in the flood area.

## *Give People the Sense That They Are Part of Something Important*

I do not often hear from the top managers I interview that the most important thing in their career is making money. Talented people are generally well compensated. And if they are offered more money from another company, their own is likely to match it. The thing I hear more in my interviews is "I want to be engaged in what's going on in the company." Most of us spend the biggest chunk of our time working, and if we don't think what we are doing is important or meaningful, then dissatisfaction or depression is bound to settle in. An employee is the most vulnerable when he is the least happy in his work. Connect their jobs to something bigger. "Mission" has become an overworked word, but where the company is going and how it is going to get there can be a very personal issue for managers. When employees view their company as a kind of family, or, better still, as a cause, then it will be hard for them to leave.

What kind of "cause"? Beating the competition to create the best products possible. That's what you have to do to succeed. Get everyone engaged in that fight. I've seen a great CEO impress upon the guy who waxes the floors how important it is to the company's success when a customer walks into the building and sees clean, shiny floors. You cannot overcommunicate your vision for the company. People are thirsty for a sense of where the company is going. "Are we going global?" "How fast?" "Are we doing it by acquisition or organically?" "How will it affect me?" Shoot for products that make clients' jaws drop. When customers look at a new product and say, "Wow, that is so much better than what anyone else has!" that gets people in an organization very excited. If you make everyone part of a successful mission, it will be hard for them to walk away, particularly to join a competitor. I have interviewed managers who have become so much a part of the culture of IBM, for example, that they cannot imagine themselves working for another computer company. "This is the ideal job you're offering me, and the money is terrific," candidates have confessed to me, "but I just can't see myself working for a company that I've been competing against for twenty years."

Some companies are even in a position to help change the world. The advent of the cellular phone has made it possible for developing countries to leap into the twenty-first century without the prohibitive costs of laying traditional telephone lines. HP's new "e-clusion" program, which will donate a billion dollars' worth of equipment and services to Third World countries to help farmers, entrepreneurs, and government agencies to become more productive, is bound to appeal to talented young managers who think a career with a Fortune 50 company ought to be about more than making enough money for early retirement.

### *Communicate Your Vision Nonstop*

Once you have your mission straight, get the word out. The best companies get their top people together constantly in informal settings—at breakfast meetings, luncheons, off-site retreats—to discuss the company's challenges and goals. Good leaders are usually out in front of their organizations. But the best leaders have ways of letting their people catch up. They know how to get the dialogue going. (And they know, as well, that once an idea is passed around a room, it becomes the group's idea.)

Get in front of your people to talk—and listen. Any leader who talks to his people about what he wants to do and where he wants to go will not only create a buzz around himself, but his subordinates will feel that they, too, are part of the leadership team. "Hey, he knows my name." "He actually asked me to write my idea up in a memo." "He cares about my opinions." If your people are talented and worth keeping, then you should care about what they have to say. After all, it is the future of your company.

### Get People Engaged in Problem Solving

You want people to be innovative, but you also should let them make decisions about their ideas. "Here's the problem." "Do you see it the same way I do?" "What do you think?" "How do we take advantage of this opportunity?" "What are our options?" When you get people involved in problem solving, they will also be committed to the solution. The more commitment that managers feel for what's happening at the company and the people involved, the harder it is for them to leave.

### Get Them Committed to Their Subordinates and Customers

Part of making jobs more meaningful is clarifying that the people doing them are working toward something beyond the bottom line or their own self-interest. Turn the company upside down so that it is clear to your managers that they are also serving others—their subordinates and the customer. Part of a good manager's job is to help others get their jobs done successfully, to create levels of high performance and productivity, and to be able to solve problems for the customer.

While searching for a candidate for the CEO position at Hewlett-Packard in 1999, I talked to several of the top CEOs in America who were naturals for the HP job. But they wouldn't bite because of the commitment they had made to the people who they had gone out and hired to work for them. In a sense, they had created their own retention program by creating obligations to the people they had brought in under them.

### Identify Your Best People—and Be Nice to Them

And I mean more than sending "Happy Birthday" e-mails. Get creative about letting your best managers know how much you appreciate their work and support. Be respectful, and show it by doing little things. Send a letter home so that the person's significant other can see it, so that he or she can know that all the hard work and time away from family has been noticed. I know top executives who always have something in their drawer to send off, a funny award or personal touch that people might value. Such efforts do not have to be Hollywood-extreme—Christmas in Aspen, or new Land Rovers—but they must be genuine and meaningful.

### Be Especially Nice to Your New Employees

People tend to remember how they were treated in their most vulnerable moments, and what is scarier than being young, inexperienced, and into your first weeks on a new job?

Like many successful new-economy companies, Cisco Systems has grown by acquiring new companies. Buying companies is also a classic way of acquiring new talent, and no company is better at integrating new people into its company and holding on to them than Cisco, where new employees get a "sponsor" to help them acclimate. By cultivating your new people, you create loyalty. And loyalty is what makes it hard for people to leave, no matter how attractive the offer.

### Create a Safe Environment That Allows Mistakes

Innovation is not likely to happen if people get hammered for every failure. You must create an atmosphere on the job in which employees can feel that it is okay to feel vulnerable. You want them to be able to come to you and say, "I made a mistake." Your response ought to be, "Okay, what did you learn? What are we going to do differently next time?"

We tend to learn very little from success and a lot from failure. I believe that's because we don't often analyze our successes, but when we flop, we stew about it, run it over and over in our minds. "How could this have happened?" "What could I have done differently?" Discussing failures and mistakes frankly can be a win-win situation all around: as an understanding leader, you will encourage your people to be creative; as a practical boss, you are also making sure a costly mistake does not get repeated. To err is human, but erring the same way twice is grounds for getting the boot. No good manager gets points for putting up with constant screwups.

### Be the Company's Top Recruiter

Make sure your best people know what their next job is. You cannot do enough for your real performers, the people you have nightmares about losing. Get to know them so well that it will not be uncomfortable to check in on them regularly to find out how things are going. Be clear about what their next challenge and career opportunity will be. Discuss with them what they will need to get there, and when it might happen. "Are things going okay?" "Do you think we're making progress?" "Are you comfortable?"

This kind of communication has not been common in the business world where the model of the distant boss has been the norm. But to hold on to good people, you have to make a huge effort to ensure they are happy, challenged, and motivated. And every once in a while it might not hurt to take your best people up to the corner office with the view and tell them that someday this may all be theirs. Outline their future in the company, even a scenario of succession: "Today you're executive vice president, a year from now you will be my COO, and two years after that, if all goes well, you're going to become CEO, and I will be the chairman."

In 1999, Polaroid's VP of human resources looked around and suddenly noticed that many of the company's most talented and experienced managers were gone, either through retirement or defections to Internet start-ups. The company quickly began developing and promoting its young stars, who were now ready to play their part in Polaroid's succession plans. What better way to motivate your young drivers and leaders than by placing a big job in their sights? If they do not know what possibilities are theirs, if you do not feed their dreams and excite their imaginations, another company will step up and do just that. (Just don't put it in writing.)

### When the Challenge Runs Out, Move Them Up

You have to be ready to promote your best people faster than other companies can recruit them. If you have the right talent, you will grow, and a thriving company should have plenty of opportunities (and compensation) to go around. If you are creating more products, you will need more product managers, more directors of sales and marketing. Examine the résumés of the top management of companies with the best retention rates, places like IBM, GE, Goldman Sachs, Continental, Amgen, and Sun Microsystems, where people stay forever: the list of their different jobs in the company is astonishing. One of the men in line for Jack Welch's job at GE—James McNerney—worked for GE Capital, GE Information Services, and then ran GE Aircraft Engines, GE lighting, and GE Asia-Pacific. Eighteen years of success, and he didn't even get the big job!

Find the superstars and nurture them. You must be constantly reevaluating your bench strength—people who've grown up in the company who surprise you, newcomers you've brought in from other companies. Be willing to move them up, maybe even faster than usual. To keep its young people and to replace the top managers who are retiring or moving on to second careers, Polaroid is promoting managers who in the old days (1998) would have had to wait another three years. You've got to be able to take somebody who's a manager today and jump them up two levels, past director to vice president.

### Have a List of Top Posts Earmarked for In-House Talent

Chief operating officer, for example. Headhunters will tell you that the hardest position to recruit into is COO, mainly because of expectations. Most companies expect the COO to be the CEO eventually, and so they look for a particularly strong candidate. But in this Talent Economy, any candidate strong enough to *be* a CEO can *find* a CEO's position. There will always be members of the existing management team who think they ought to be COO. Bringing in an outsider can have the effect of "antibodies" attacking a healthy system: "He hasn't been here for thirty years—that was *my* job," say several managers. They leave, and so do many of the people who preferred the old way of doing things.

But promoting a current general manager to COO with the intent of grooming him or her for the CEO job can work very well. When the succession finally takes place, employees already know the new CEO. More important, talented young managers see that they have a good chance of being rewarded if they stay.

### Get Rid of Those Who Drag the Organization Down

This is the hard part. But it is crucial. Winners want to work with winners. You have to lose the bottom 10 to 20 percent of performers who are depressing the rest of the organization. You don't want others thinking, "Why am I working so hard when that slacker makes the same amount of money as I do?" Nor do you want to have your good people wondering whether they're in the right company. General Electric is constantly grading its managers on a scale of one to ten. During periodical reviews, anyone with a five or under is a candidate for the door. Before he was boosted to chairman of CBS, Mel Karmazin ran the network's chain of radio stations and was a notoriously stern taskmaster. He set a 40 percent annual increase minimum for his salespeople. Those who didn't make that number were automatically gone.

Firing people is a miserable job and maybe Karmazin's bar was set unreasonably high. But you have to set some standards of managerial excellence and then figure out how to deliver the bad news to those dragging down your company. And you needn't worry about your notoriety as a manager who likes to fire people. In 1996, AT&T fired 30,000 employees, earning then-CEO Robert

Allen the cover of *Newsweek*—with the headline "Corporate Killers." Yet Allen's reputation as a great CEO followed him into retirement a year later. Not long after Jack Welch took over General Electric he cut costs and fired thousands of people, earning him the nickname "Neutron Jack." By the time he announced his resignation, twenty years later, *Fortune* was calling him "the leading management revolutionary of the century." If you can't bear to fire people, hire someone who can. The good news is that you can use those resources to hire better managers.

### Be Clear About Who the Enemy Is

Your colleagues, no matter how annoying, are not the enemy. Inside the company, we are all in this together—a team. The enemy is the competition, or anything that keeps you from beating the competition. So the enemy could also be within the organization in the form of a poor product, bad quality, or weak strategy. The best leaders create teams and goals that excite employees, the market, and the financial community. If your talent is excited about being on a team that's going somewhere (or solving the problems that will open the way to success), they'll be more likely to stay.

### Ask Your Team Members What They Appreciate Most

I recently interviewed a woman for an administrative assistant's job in my own office and learned as much from talking to her as I have in many of my interviews with CEOs. Frankly, I am now so used to grilling top managers and CEOs that I was unsure what to ask her. I decided to begin with one of the questions I often ask candidates for top management: "What was your favorite job?"

She said she had really liked her previous job, before she had to relocate for family reasons. "My boss took an interest in me," she explained. "He made sure that I had the right sort of experiences and was able to improve and grow in the job. And that made it fun for me." I thought about that for a while and realized that it's the same kind of answer the best CEOs give. Most successful managers have had a coach or mentor, someone a little bit older who early in their career took a special interest in them and helped them get better at their job or prepare for a better job. If that mentor is you, then you will be more likely to keep your best people from leaving.

### *Offer Training and Education*

Ambitious people want to improve their skills. And if, as they say, knowledge is power, why not increase your company's potential by encouraging your top people to increase their knowledge? For decades, Fortune 500 companies have been paying tuition for employees who want to return to school or learn skills that would improve their on-job performance. United Technologies, for example, pays tuition for employees and gives them stock if they graduate. Paine Webber pays for New York University to send business professors to the company's New Jersey headquarters and teach night courses for about twenty of the firm's most promising young employees. "This is totally related to the tight labor market," said the Paine Webber executive in charge of career development. "We want to make this as convenient as possible for them." That is the kind of attitude that instills company loyalty.

## *Let Your People Know That No Job Is a Small Job*

Every manager can be an owner—if he thinks his job is worth his time and effort. No matter where you are in the organization, CEO or manager, you should be telling people how important their work is. In the process, you should be encouraging them to make that job better, to be more creative about their work. Why should anyone do a better job, if the boss has not made it clear that he cares? Someone who ran a small personal care products company once told me a story about an assembly-line glitch where the end product was coming out with an unsightly foam on top. The manufacturing department spent weeks analyzing the problem and concluded that the machinery would have to be retooled to melt the foam—at a cost of $30,000. One of the guys on the line had an idea, rushed home, and returned with his wife's hair dryer. He plugged it in, set it up at the end of the assembly line, turned it on, and signaled for the line to start. The hair dryer melted the foam, saving the company a bundle. Would that guy have volunteered a solution if no one had ever encouraged him to be part of a team and speak his mind? I doubt it. Did he feel that he was a valued employee after his coup? You bet he did, and the company rewarded him generously for his creativity. Engage your people in their jobs. Find out what they think, what they'd like to improve, what they think the company should be doing differently.

## *Never Underestimate the Appeal of Job Security*

When talent starts analyzing the pros and cons of moving on, you want to make sure the "con" list is long and annoying. Smart executives know that every move involves a risk. By now, smart young managers know that not every Internet start-up is Amazon or AOL. (Indeed, even Amazon and AOL are shadows of their former selves, at least from Wall Street's point of view.) You want to keep your best people focused on the advantages of the opportunities and security of your company. I heard one chief executive of a traditional company joke about framing copies of all those magazine cover stories that appeared at the end of 2000—"Dot-Coms Go Bust," "Unplugging the New Economy," and so on—and hanging them on the walls of the company cafeteria as a reminder of the risks of leaving the mother ship.

### Institute Periodic Reassessments of Your Retention Strategies

Even when you have done all of the above and have achieved what you and your employees agree is a kind of corporate nirvana, you will have to keep reassessing your company's retention strategy. Pitney Bowes, for example, thought it was covered. For years the company had managed to keep its turnover rate within the "normal" range and had made sure that its staff was not skewed too old and thus vulnerable to a quick talent gap when too many people retired. Nevertheless, after a routine reassessment of its talent pool in 2000, Pitney's human resources department detected a shortage of executives ready to step up into general manager positions. The company quickly identified thirty up-and-comers, compared their strengths and weaknesses to the company's most senior executives, and then put the young managers through a year's worth of programs designed to help each of them mirror the best of Pitney Bowes's top management. The company has also identified an even smaller group of talented managers and assigned them mentors from other divisions who will help them boost their skills in their weak areas and educate them about different areas of the business. When positions open up, Pitney will already have a long line of managers on the bench ready to move into them.

And no matter how hard you work at keeping employees happy, some of them are bound to leave for what they think is the offer of a lifetime. Don't let them. Make them a counteroffer they cannot refuse.

## CHAPTER 6

## *Talent Is Worth Fighting For*

Your best manager walks into your office, closes the door, and announces, "We gotta talk." It is every boss's nightmare—and it will hurt even more when it happens after you have done everything in your power to create the most positive, flexible, autonomous work environment possible for nurturing talent. It has certainly happened to me. Several years ago, for example, I heard through the rumor mill that one of the most promising people in the company was unhappy and ready to make a move. Our clients were getting better, we had more searches for higher-level positions, and the firm was making money. We had finally gotten the company focused on recruiting high-caliber talent, and now one of our true up-and-comers was halfway out the door.

But no company is immune to losing talent. In today's competitive environment, an average performer in your company might be considered a "hot prospect." Truly exceptional performers are likely to have three to four companies pursuing them at any given time. In the past few years, we've helped clients recruit top managers from AT&T, IBM, Dell, Hewlett-Packard, and Office Depot. If the stars in those kinds of companies are poachable, how do companies like yours and mine hold on to our talent?

Frankly, it's a challenge. The competition has done everything in its power to persuade them to jump ship. The CEO is taking them for drinks, inviting them to play golf at Pebble Beach. Recruiters are offering to put together compensation packages that will up their salaries and compensate for lost stock options. In fact, they have done all the things I have been advising you to do in this book to recruit talent. And if your guy has been professionally recruited, the headhunter will have coached him to get out your office door before you've even recovered from the shock of his resignation. Over a twenty-five-year career, I myself have instructed literally thousands of executives on how to make a quick, clean exit, without tears. Your guy has been told to announce his resignation and make it clear that his mind has been made up. He has been told to be polite but firm. "You and the company have been great to me, but my mind is made up," he will say, diplomatically. He will explain that it is nothing personal, he respects you and the company, he never thought this moment would come, but—and I guarantee this will come next—he will add in a tone as serious as he can muster, "This is an opportunity of a lifetime."

You can fight back. You cannot afford not to fight. The loss of productive, high-octane employees can have a significant impact on any leading company's success. The loss of even one high performer can send ripples through an entire organization. And even if you can match the talent you have lost with an equally talented

new player, it could cost *three times* the salary of the person you
have lost. My colleagues and I spend our days and nights trying to
recruit people away from top companies, and our experience indicates that most organizations are deep in denial about their vul-
nerability on the talent front. A recent survey of 551 large U.S.
companies only confirms what we have seen: 54 percent did not
have a formal strategy for retaining their best people. This is mad-
ness. Would you want the competition to steal your best customer?
Letting them steal your best talent is equally catastrophic. Every
company needs to have a plan in place to counter raids on talent.

As soon as I found out that one of my best people was itching to
leave, I moved quickly to find out what was wrong before he got
picked off. I was lucky that he had not been shy about letting his
colleagues know what bothered him about the company. Immediately, I sought him out and asked him to tell me what was wrong.
His main complaint was that he did not think our best resources—
assistants, researchers, data on clients and candidates—were being
fairly distributed. It is a common problem in smaller companies,
where everyone must share a finite number of resources. Senior
managers will tend to horde certain backup staff, leaving younger
people frustrated and bitter about operating under a handicap. He
gave me a detailed explanation of what was wrong—and thus the
ammunition for a strategy to keep him. I decided to make him part
of the solution. "You come up with some ideas for how to solve
this, show us how they'll work, and we'll let you run with it." He
identified the areas where he thought he could make a difference,
and the firm agreed to set up an "experimental work group" to
apply his ideas. There was no more talk about leaving. He himself
fixed the very problems that annoyed him, made life easier and

more equitable for the rest of us, and proceeded to design and implement innovations in other important areas of our business. To show our gratitude, we made him a partner.

And so hearts can be won and minds can be changed. In a career of trying to persuade talent to make a move, I have come up against some effective counterstrategies by companies eager to headhunter-proof themselves. The person resigning has been advised to be a block of ice in the face of all appeals to reconsider. Your goal is to put some cracks into that ice and then melt them down into a born-again loyal employee wondering why they even considered leaving a boss and company as wonderful as you and yours. The main advantage you have over the competition is that you already have a relationship. Their decision to leave was probably a tough one, and the prospect of announcing it to you face-to-face has been even more agonizing. Exploit that discomfort. Do not let them out the door without a discussion. Any counterstrategy will have to be shaped to fit the specific case at hand. The first thing you must do is shake off the initial shock and start buying some time.

## STAGE ONE: SOWING DOUBT

### *Stay Cool*

Yes, you are ticked off that this person whom you've pampered, promoted, and treated like a son is dumping you. Take a deep breath and focus your emotional response on figuring out how to change his mind. Again, think of this as a client or customer announcing that they are taking their business elsewhere. What are the odds of changing a customer's mind if your first response is to start screaming or throwing things? Keeping this manager is equally as important.

### Start Asking Questions

You want to learn as much as you can about why they're leaving so that you can create a strategy for keeping them. To do that, you've got to engage them, get them to open up about their reasons for deciding to leave. You have to break down barriers and try to rebuild trust. In short, you have to start asking questions, lots of them. Such as:

- What made you accept a phone call from a search firm to begin with?
- How do you feel about our company?
- What was the problem here?
- What should we have fixed so that you wouldn't have resigned?
- If this has been a tough decision for you, what made it so tough?
- What really excites you about this new job?
- How do you know that what they are telling you is for real?
- Have you done your due diligence on them?
- If so, what did you find out?
- Are you sure this new company is the right place for you?
- If all things were equal—the same job, the same dough—would you stay?
- Is there something we can fix so that you will stay? (Be careful with this one. Save it for the right moment.)
- If we can fix it, will you stay?

I recommend having this group of questions written down on a separate yellow pad or whatever you generally use for taking notes in meetings. Make sure this "resignation pad" is within reach in your desk. Before the dreaded meeting, review the questions. Even if someone springs a resignation on you, you'll be able to grab it— "You don't mind if I take some notes?" They will never know that you always keep your own arsenal of counterweapons handy.

### Listen Hard

Don't be arrogant or defensive. Let them vent a little. They are bound to be nervous and uncomfortable. Avoiding confrontation and striving for understanding and sympathy will remind them what a good boss you have been. Encourage them to be frank. And then listen carefully for the kind of information that will be useful in creating a strategy to get them to reverse their decision.

### Try a Little Magnanimity

Take the high road by making it clear that you have appreciated their work and care about their future. Chances are that earlier in your career you, too, made a decision to move on. Sometimes change can be good. "I just want you to be sure you make the right move." Point out that you think they are talented enough to be successful in a lot of companies. "But is this the right one? We need you. The people who work for you need you."

### The Right Kind of Discussion Might Raise Some Doubts

All of us have taken jobs where promises were made and then broken. Even when an employer is sincere, things change—the stock market dips, interest rates go up, the economy falters, a competitor gets lucky, another division of the company or subsidiary goes into free fall, canceling out current business plans, and so on and so on. When executives are recruited, they are likely to have seen the new company in its best light, its top management on its best behavior. Your job is to get them to reconsider the competition under a dark cloud. Zero in on what they know about the new company. Get them wondering if they've done enough research about this new job.

- What do you know of people who have left the company recently?
- What do the people who have left say about the company?
- Have you talked to any of their customers?

### *Ask Some Probing Questions About the Other Company*

The goal is to get them to consider their future employer without the smiley face they doubtless saw during the big interview. Remind them that they are comparing your company, which they know from all sides (including the downside), to only the brightest picture of the company they are moving to. Here are some additional questions that will help people think harder about the other guys:

- It's a big job they're giving you. Why do you think it was available?
- Did your predecessor leave? If so, why?
- Was he pushed? (And thus the implication: You could be pushed, too.)
- Why do people stagnate in that company and not move up?

- What do you see as your next job there?
- How do they provide autonomy?
- What level was the person who came to sell you on the job? (Implying that if it wasn't the top person, then the job might not be so important to him.)
- Money and job title aside, why do you think this new company will be a better place?

### Try to Put Them in Your Shoes

All of the above questions are fishing for answers that will help you come up with ways to help reverse their decision to leave. Don't be afraid to get specific. For example:

- What's really important to you in your career right now?
- What didn't we do six months ago that might have avoided this?
- What are the problems that you could have fixed?
- What should I be doing to fix them?
- What would you have done differently if you had been given more autonomy?
- If you were me, what would you do to keep someone as good as you?
- What would it take for you to stay?
- What should we be talking about?
- How important is money to you?
- How important is your title?

At this point in the meeting, you might run into a wall of silence. They have been coached to make the break as quick and clean as possible. "This is just about business." Your job is to keep it as messy and as personal as possible. You have cultivated their careers, turned them into stars. They owe you. But you can still shape the rest of the conversation in business terms. "Okay, you're leaving, but you at least owe me the benefit of your experience here." Let them play the consultant, while they continue to give you more ammunition for your counteroffensive. These questions will help:

- What do we have to do to keep people like you?
- If our whole business was focused on being able to make sure we kept our best people—namely, people like you—what should we do to restructure ourselves so that this doesn't happen again?

By now your strategy should be taking shape in your mind, and you can let them out the door—but not off the hook. No matter how much they insist that their decision is final, get them to give you time to make a counteroffer. Here I advise being shameless. "You know, you've been here a long time, Charlie. You and I, we've known each other for a while. I've heard everything you've been saying about why you've decided to leave, but I'd like you to do one last thing for me." Exploit your past relationship, do not let them forget how their talent was able to flourish in your company, that you have played a role in making them attractive to the competition. All you want is one last favor: "Don't make a final decision until I have had a chance to talk to the board and others in the company and respond to you. Can you at least do that for me?" Few people will be hard-hearted enough to turn down that kind of request, regardless of how well they have been coached. Ask for forty-eight hours to respond.

## STAGE TWO: CREATING AN EFFECTIVE
## COUNTEROFFER

Central to any effort to keep your talent on the home team is the notion that *people work for people.* No matter how attractive a new job looks on paper, no matter how appealing novelty will always be, no matter the prospect of adventure and challenge, all that can implode in a flash if the human connections at the other end do not mesh. The wild card is the other people, their ambitions, their envy, their craziness. Keep stressing that. Your talented manager has done well in your company—has friends there, commitments. Build on that goodwill and those relationships.

### Examine All Your Alternatives

Before you waste a lot of energy putting together a counteroffer, you should be absolutely sure that they are worth keeping. Consider how long it might take to replace them and the costs. Evaluate how much value they have really added to your company. Once you confirm that a counteroffer is worth it, you should begin putting together the information that can help you make your case for staying irresistible. Find their friends in the company, the people they might have discussed their decision with.

### Flattery Will Get You Everywhere

If they are as talented as you and the competition believe, it should not be hard to lay on the praise. Maybe they have never known how much you have appreciated their contribution. It is time to make amends. Put together a list of things you've liked, such as special skills, projects they have completed, numbers they have made, their triumphs. The key here is to get them reengaged with the future of the company and with their continued role in it. Make it very clear how central they are to the success of the company.

Details will not only strengthen your argument against resignation but also impress them with your extensive knowledge of their work. "If you had left in the middle of the project we did two years ago—the A711—it would have been a disaster. We're now deep into project A712, and if we lose you, we're bound to lose other people, lose the customers who were counting on you, and thus lose revenue." Such anecdotes have double power: they flatter him while also making him feel guilty about leaving.

Remind them how much their departure will affect colleagues and staffers (or even the stock price). One of the most common reasons I get from executives not interested in being recruited is that they themselves have hired a loyal team and would feel like a traitor if they left the company at this time. So don't be shy about pointing out how important their work is. "If you were to leave right now, it would be catastrophic for everybody." Inquire about what kind of strategy or new vision it would take to get them excited about the company again.

### Set Up a Metric for a Change That They Can Manage

You want to persuade him that his future role in the company will be different—and you'll have to have some specifics in mind. By now you should have a very good idea of why he's leaving and what the other company has offered. You have asked about what he didn't like. Now give him the kind of job or responsibility or autonomy or resources he has always wanted, and make it clear that "I will help you make it happen."

### Gang Up on Them

Put together a team of people from inside the company who know and care about her—peers as well as bosses—and work out a common, two-stage retention strategy. First: one-on-one meetings between these people and their colleague who's decided to resign. Second: joint meetings between the entire team and her. Make sure your colleagues know that this is red-alert time. Again, pose the emergency in a way that everyone can understand its importance—i.e., it's as if we were losing our best client or facing an immediate downturn in revenue.

Before anyone makes a move, rehearse what the one-on-one meetings should be like. Be sure everyone is on the same page, that your goals are clear. Same for the joint meeting. Planning ahead is crucial. Make sure everyone is clear about what to say and how to handle the conversation, especially with regard to her reasons for leaving. Be careful about being too overwhelming or intimidating. You're supposed to be changing her mind, not scaring her out the door. This should be a discussion between old friends and colleagues, not a Star Chamber or police third degree. Another variation is to bring them into a meeting with the four or five people they work most closely with, including subordinates. Warning: what people say has to be genuine. If it seems staged or if people seem to be acting, you are merely presenting one more reason to leave.

### Risk Your Secret Weapon

If nothing seems to be working, it may be time to live dangerously—and call the spouse. Yes, it is risky. But you can assume that the competition has already talked to the husband or wife, if only in an effort to smooth out the relocation details. What to say? Tell them how important their spouses are to the company. Surely they have been thinking a lot about the change, the effects it will have on the kids, the family, their own career. They are bound to be concerned about long-term financial security, so play on those concerns. Assure them that their spouse has a job for life at your company. You might even luck out. Maybe they've already raised some of these same concerns. The husband or wife might have reluctantly agreed to give up their job for this opportunity. If you can match the offer plus cancel the stress on the spouse, you may have picked up an ally.

### Thinking Through the Counteroffer

Don't be too quick to whip out your checkbook. As we have seen, when talent is looking to move, they are usually after more responsibility and bigger challenges. Amazingly, just as I was drafting this chapter I got a call from the editor of this book, announcing that he was leaving to take another job. I laughed at the irony of the situation and read him the title of this chapter. "It's not about money," he assured me. He simply had a dream offer to develop projects for a well-known movie producer. He also told me that his boss at Random House had made the only counteroffer that could have caused him to think twice about his decision. (I'll tell you what it was when we get to that stage of the process.)

If you've asked the right questions and listened to the answers, you should be clear about why they want to leave. It is now time to devise your final arguments for why it is critical that the company not lose them. If money can help, make it clear that whatever their current compensation package is, it is now cancelled and negotiable. This should make it clear how important they are to you. (Don't make a counteroffer over the phone. I have tried to do this when someone in my own company has resigned. It was a bad idea and it didn't work. Face-to-face. You can bet the people who are recruiting him are not doing it by phone.)

### Be Prepared to Eat Some Humble Pie

Concede that you have made a big mistake. "We've gotten so busy, maybe we haven't been giving you the recognition that you deserve." Admit that the news that they were leaving not only was a shock but also opened your eyes to their contribution to the company's success, and that you're eager to increase that role—if they would just give you the chance to prove it.

I know it is not easy to eat humble pie. But the goal is to keep them. You like them; you value their talent. They like your company and appreciate what you have done for their career. It is not as if either side is lying. So why not exploit the truth?

### The Bottom Line

In spite of the insistence that "It's not about the money," I have never seen an important retention happen without increased compensation on the table. Some cash always helps. Stock options, too. How much is too much? You definitely have to listen to what the competition is saying. Their figure is likely to be an eye-opener—maybe even more money than you're paying anyone else in your organization doing the equivalent (or maybe even a higher) job. Nevertheless, it is important to snap out of that sticker shock and put the money into perspective. If the studies are right about top performers being exponentially more productive than their colleagues, if it is true that the cost of replacing good executives is triple their salary, a major compensation hike might actually be a bargain. Or an investment. When clients resist the kind of money I think it will take to recruit someone they want, I often suggest that they consider a talented manager's value to a company over the length of a career. Amortizing the financial package over the next five or ten years is a useful way to remove its sting.

### Increase Their Prospects

Most people are unlikely to leave a good position unless they are being offered a better one. As we have seen, talent is not interested in moving sideways. They have their dreams, and sometimes it takes another company (or a headhunter) to recognize their value and potential. So look at this challenge as a wake-up call. They may have been around so long and become so essential to your operation that you have begun to take them for granted, something they were more likely to notice than you. If the competition sees them in a bigger job with a better title, then you will have to match that offer—even if it means reorganizing the company's top management structure.

### Find Out What Their Dreams Are—and Fulfill Them

After my editor announced that he was leaving publishing for a new opportunity acquiring literary projects for a successful movie producer—and "it wasn't about money"—his boss came back at him with what he confided to me was "the only thing that could make me think twice about leaving—time." Realizing that this editor was writing plays on the side and that a musical he'd cowritten had had a workshop production, Random House's editor in chief offered him the choice of a sabbatical or a three-day-a-week deal that would allow him to pursue his creative work outside book publishing. "That was an incredibly innovative—and generous—offer," he said, clearly flattered by his boss's efforts to keep him.

My book agent, Jim Levine, fared a lot better with a similar offer. When one of his most productive and experienced agents announced in the summer that she wanted to "take a sabbatical" beginning in January, he replied, "You've got the solution, but I don't know what the problem is." Though she loved her work, she explained that she was frustrated at spending all her time nurturing other people's creativity without any time left to pursue her own art and writing projects. Having built a successful literary agency while also managing to write several books, Levine understood her dilemma; he also thought she would be a better agent if she found the right balance between the agency's work and her own. "Why wait until January?" Levine said. "Let's start next week." He immediately proposed that instead of a sabbatical she cut back her work week to four days; if that didn't give her enough time, he was willing to have her work three days a week and adjust her client load accordingly. "Let's treat it as an experiment and see what combination works."

The four-day scheme seemed to work fine, and when she wondered about spending more time in California, where her boyfriend lived, Levine switched gears again and suggested she set up a West Coast office for his New York City–based firm. "For my kind of work, it's all about talent," explains Levine. "Realizing that I could not afford to lose such a high performer, I was willing to do just about anything to keep her happy. To have her producing at even half capacity was better than losing her." Levine also calculated that setting her up with a high-speed modem connection, a fax, a copy machine, and a few return plane tickets from California would cost him only about $5,000. The agent was soon spending a quarter of her time in New York, and over the next year was as productive as ever. In the meantime, she co-wrote and published two of her own books. She is now back working full time as an agent, but Levine is ready to adjust again in order to maximize her talents as an agent-author. A definite win-win situation—all due to a quick and creative counteroffer.

### The Bad News

In my experience, when talented managers have made the decision to accept a big offer, the odds of keeping them are fifty-fifty, or less. But if a certain manager is as good as you (and the competition) think, a fifty-fifty shot at reversing the decision to leave is certainly worth the effort, not to mention some serious dollars. Moreover, if it is fifty-fifty from the get-go, you are likely to increase those odds by devising the kind of counteroffer that makes staying in a familiar situation more attractive than taking a flyer with a new company and working under a new boss (who is nowhere near the prince among men that you are). The person who wanted to leave my company really only wanted to be doing more with us. Once I found out what he thought was missing in my organization and put him in charge of a solution, the idea of leaving disappeared. We both have been benefiting from the change ever since.


## But Who Knows?

Even if in the face of the most generous (and ingenious) counter-offers you can devise, they still decide to leave, there is always the possibility that this great, new job will not be so wonderful after all. Many companies are now discovering that keeping their best people can also mean luring them back *after* they've left. Following the Wall Street slide of April 2000, many large companies stifled their bitterness and began getting in touch with their refugees. Andersen Consulting sent a letter to nearly 3,000 recently departed former employees informing them that if they missed their old company, Andersen missed them, too, and would welcome them back. The letter even promised the kind of extra equity that had seduced many into the dot-com world. PricewaterhouseCoopers encouraged employees to call friends and colleagues who had left to ask them "to come home."

So when you've tried everything to get them to stay and they leave, wish them well—in case the job blows up in their face and they want to come home. Talented managers will hardly be offended by your efforts to keep them from resigning. My Random House editor told me that because his boss did everything in her power to keep him, should this next big step in his career falter, "I would certainly consider returning—if she'd have me." Three months later he was back at Random House working on this book again. His adventure in the movie business had revealed to him how much he loved book publishing. "I realized I was a book editor at heart," he explained. "And I kept hearing the words of my Random House boss in my ears—'Sometimes you have to leave home to find home.' In the end, that intuitive understanding and trust made me want to come home."

### Some Advice for Next Time

In a Talent Economy, where your best people will be pursued constantly, shouldn't you be ready for the inevitable? I would advise against trying to reinvent the wheel every time someone gets a good job offer. Establish a kind of counteroffer SWAT team that will go into action as soon as the word gets out that an offer is on the table. Select a group of your best executives, including your top salespeople, who are genuinely pumped about the company and are extremely committed to its future growth. They tend to be the managers who spot talent and bring it into the company, and they may actually be the ones who recruited the manager who is about to give notice.

Being able to move fast is bound to increase your chances of persuading good people not to leave. If you already have an experienced emergency retention team in place, you will be able to aim it at your wayward talent in a flash. I would also suggest that this retention team be relatively young—the same age as the managers most likely to be recruited. As anyone who has been to high school knows, peer pressure is a powerful thing. Also, the very existence of such a team proves the company's commitment to talent and is likely to help bond its members to the company. If you've spent a couple of years helping to talk your colleagues out of jumping ship, how easy will it be to leave when *you* get an offer?

### The Best Weapon for Keeping Talent—Success

Before your talent walks into your office and says, "We gotta talk," someone has had to convince him that the opportunity of a life-time lies outside your company. The companies with the lowest turnover rates, such as General Electric, Goldman Sachs, South-west Airlines, and scores of other "most admired" American companies, have created a work environment where hardly anyone wants to leave. Losing good people should make you work even harder at creating that environment where people hardly ever think of leaving. Every time you lose someone, you should learn more about what you ought to be doing to prevent it from happening again. Talented people, as we have seen, thrive on success. If you can convince your talent that their best future lies with you, then you might just avoid scrambling to keep them.

PART II

# TALENT—BECOMING IT

## CHAPTER 7

# Building Your Talent Quotient—and Your Career

It does seem that some people have the CEO gene—brains that operate at megahertz speeds, personalities that dominate a room, and the stamina of a triathlete. They are born leaders. Fortunately for us normal humans, there are many routes to the top, and not all of them have to run through the Harvard Business School or management training programs at IBM, GE, or Goldman Sachs. There is plenty of evidence (and comfort) in the résumés of some of the most respected chief executives in U.S. business. How much education is enough? Gordon Bethune, the CEO of Continental Airlines, dropped out of high school. Surely you need a technical background to rise to the top in the high-tech industry, right? Carly Fiorina majored in medieval history and philosophy at Stanford and began her business career as an account executive at AT&T. And you better not make a mistake in that first big job you get. In his first job, Jack Welch accidentally blew up a warehouse. My first foray as an entrepreneur was to create a natural-food business that was history within nine months.

As someone who is not a naturally gifted business executive, it is my pleasure to inform you that people like us are running success-ful companies all over the world. We are extremely lucky people, but we have also worked incredibly hard at planning our careers, working later than the person in the next cubicle, and working smarter (even though our neighbor might be more gifted intellec-tually). Above all, the people I know who have scrambled their way to success make sure they learn from the best performers in their organizations. They found mentors and created large and ever-expanding personal networks that helped them at every stage of their careers.

Great careers do not happen, people build them, and often from the most unlikely material. Continental's Gordon Bethune wanted to join the Navy because he hated high school. The Navy tested him and immediately ordered him into technical school to study aircraft maintenance. He became the best mechanic in the Navy and its youngest peacetime chief petty officer. Moving to Boeing, he rose to run one of the company's most important factories and then got the call to be COO of Continental in 1994. Before the end of the year, his boss quit, and Bethune was named CEO of the struggling airline. It's not struggling anymore. After Stanford, Carly Fiorina switched her educational goals from medieval stud-ies to business, studying at MIT and the University of Maryland Business School. When I began recruiting her for the Hewlett-Packard job, one of the first things she made clear to me was "I am not a technologist." But throughout her career she has been effec-tive at listening to people who are.

After the warehouse incident, Jack Welch was sure he was going to be fired. But his boss gave him another chance, and Welch has made a practice of doing the same for his employees as he built one of the most extraordinary careers (and companies) in the history of American business. My own business education has come from hitting every wall an entrepreneur can and finally realizing that as a headhunter I had access to some of the best business advice in America. All I had to do was ask my clients and the most talented managers they were trying to recruit the right questions and then pay attention.

In the previous chapters, I covered everything I have learned about how companies recognize talent, hire it, and keep it. To be recognized as talent you have to know what the people on the other side of the job interview are looking for. In short, *you have to look at yourself as if you were a headhunter*—and then work very hard to build on your strengths and remedy your weaknesses so that when you do get an interview, you will radiate the kind of quiet self-confidence and probing mind that says to the person on the other side of the desk: "You're looking at talent."

You cannot begin building an impressive career too soon.

## EDUCATE YOURSELF FOR SUCCESS

One of the biggest problems with careers is that most people end up in jobs by accident, not by planning. They take a job because it was offered and not necessarily because it was the right job to take. Or, worse, they sit around waiting for a call instead of taking their career into their own hands. A recruiter is looking for a career that is on an upward trajectory. To launch your own résumé, my advice is to start as soon as you can. If you know you want to work in business, I would even recommend planning your education around where you think the market will be by the time you will graduate from college.

In any time period, certain professions catch fire. After World War II, as the economy began to pick up speed and industry was expanding, parents advised their kids to become industrial and civil engineers. In the 1960s everyone seemed to want to go to law school, while in the seventies the M.B.A. degree seemed almost as fashionable as bell-bottoms. At some point in the 1980s, I recall the president of Yale lamenting on the op-ed page of the *New York Times* that upwards of 40 percent of the senior class had applied for jobs in investment banking. In the past decade, electrical and computer engineers were highly in demand; companies were even making offers to high school kids with a genius for programming software. In the past few years, the major consulting firms have been hiring Ph.D.s in the humanities for their creativity and diversity. ("We discovered that what we want are people who can think creatively," explained one executive. "We can teach them the business stuff.") And though it already seems like ancient history, not so long ago, ambitious B.A.s, M.B.A.s, and J.D.s streamed into the dot-coms, though not always for the right reasons. The neophyte's first task is to research which industries are growing now or are about to take off. One clear candidate for the near future in the area I know best—technology—is fiber optics. Over the next decade, there will be trillions of dollars' worth of fiber-optic cable laid across the world. Thousands of people will be hired to make it happen. Maybe you should be one of them. But you must educate yourself about the various career possibilities in that and other new industries. Many people end up succeeding in areas that they didn't even know existed when they were in school. Why wait five or ten years before you find the industry you really love? When you are evaluating a possible career, you must:

• Get on the Internet. Researching companies used to require tedious library time, pouring through business magazines and annual reports (if you could find them). All that stuff is now a mouse click away. Not only can you easily find news stories about trends in the regular and business press, but you can also check out what various think tanks are saying about the economy and industry trends. Specialized Web sites are plentiful. My company, for example, features regular stories about "hot job opportunities" based on our own research among our clients and industry observers.

• Talk to your teachers and get their take on various business trends. Ask them to introduce you to people in the industries you're interested in. After all, they're *teachers;* it is their job to be mentors to young people. Believe me, they'll be flattered by your attention. Ask them to be your coach.

• Research and study the industries that interest you to make sure you know what it is they really do. There is nothing worse than thinking you want to work for Procter & Gamble and then realizing you hate the idea of selling soap. Attend industry meetings and trade shows, even if you have to pay your way. Don't be shy. Ask lots of questions. Introduce yourself as someone who's eager to work in the industry after graduation. Ask people you meet if they'll refer you to their friends and colleagues. When I first started out in the search business, I traveled to trade shows constantly, introducing myself to people and trying to stir up search assignments. I suspect that you will be a lot better educated about the industries you're interested in than I was. I guarantee that you will make an impression.

- Practice taking risks when you're among businesspeople. Your first instinct will be to think you're being too pushy or that you'll seem foolish. But you cannot be too pushy. And I would advise that you banish all fear of making a fool of yourself. The worst that will happen is that you will learn something about the importance of relationship building in the business world.

- Look for not just the hot industry but the hot industry that will be around for a while. Get involved in local business groups so that you can meet the movers and shakers in your area. Such organizations also often invite speakers—another way to learn more about different industries and jobs.

- Apply for internships at companies in industries that appeal to you. Several summers ago, I was docking my boat in the small town of Chatham, Ontario. The dockmaster was a seventeen-year-old high school kid who was extremely helpful and congenial. It was his first job, and he was clearly good at it and clearly ambitious. I was certainly impressed. I encouraged him to talk about his interests and goals, which were in computing and software. I told him that my company needed programming help all the time and that he should keep in touch while he was in college and let me know if he wanted to spend a summer with us as an intern. He ended up doing just that, got some great experience helping us build our Web site, which helped him get a good job. Sure, it was a lucky break for him that I turned up at his dock and offered him an internship. But he had the initiative to hold me to my promise—and the talent to do the job. And what better way to explore careers than working for an executive search firm?

But the best way to become known as a talented up-and-comer is to rack up some early successes. The best odds for a shot at early success is to get a job with a market leader—an IBM or Cisco in the tech sector, for example, or a Procter & Gamble, if you're eager for a career in the personal brand business; if financial services is your dream, then a place like Citigroup would be a smart bet. Software giants such as Oracle or Microsoft will not be pushed from the top of their markets anytime soon. Companies like Nortel and Cisco will be recruiting optical network engineers for years to come.

Of course, not everybody will have the choice of a first job at one of the best companies in the world. The rest of us may find that we're limited to start-ups, early-stage companies, or turnaround situations. Don't despair. Getting a position at the right turnaround can turn into a spectacular career opportunity as well as a way to create wealth. Become a part of that legacy and recruiters will look to you merely because you played a role in that major turnaround. Promising opportunities can also be found in smaller and newer companies. The companies that dominate their markets began as start-ups. And there are always new companies with a breakthrough product or technology that emerge seemingly from nowhere to steal market share away from the giants. Cisco still owns the market in "routers," the devices that speed traffic through the Internet. But in 2000 little Juniper Networks started carving out a little piece of Cisco's router business here and another bigger piece there, quickly impressing Wall Street. A stint at Juniper during that period marked down on a résumé would catch every recruiter's eye.

To find the right career opportunity, particularly at edgy companies, you will have to become a discriminating shopper. And like any good shopper, you should begin by making a list. Twenty years ago, when I set out to get a job in the search business, I compiled a list of every search firm in the Cleveland area. I tried to get as much information about each as I could. Particularly useful were the names of those responsible for hiring new people. I began calling them to get an interview. How does a neophyte evaluate whether one company may better cultivate your career and not another? As a headhunter, I am constantly checking out companies, gauging their prospects for success, rating their talent. You have to create your own formula of research. Here is mine: plan, execute, debrief. You figure out what area you want to explore (the plan), you research and evaluate companies, talk to as many people as possible, make contacts (the execution), and finally you evaluate what worked, what didn't, and what you should do better next time (the debriefing).

### Evaluating Start-ups or Early-Stage Companies

Again, the key is to research the companies you're interested in as thoroughly and objectively as possible. Beware of hype. In the past few years, everyone in business has learned a lot about the dangers of—to borrow from Alan Greenspan—"irrational exuberance." Nowhere was irrationality more evident (at least in hindsight) than in the amazing rise and tragic fall of the dot-coms. It was gold rush fever, and even some very smart and experienced people got mangled when all those Internet start-ups came crashing down. In two decades of recruiting executives, I rarely found a talented manager willing to jump from a big and secure job at a major corporation to a start-up. The salary and bonuses at start-ups were measly by corporate standards, and the risks in betting the rest of your career on a new idea and an unproven company were daunting.

Then suddenly in the 1990s everyone in business seemed to have a friend or sister-in-law who had jumped to an Internet start-up, scoring tens of millions of dollars within weeks and hundreds of millions within months, once the company went public. Entrepreneurs and VCs were rushing top executives and young A players all over America, offering salaries and stock options that turned a lot of very smart people into greedy fools. Afraid that they would miss out on amassing the kind of wealth they had never even dreamed of until 1999, thousands of people left good jobs to help launch dot-coms built on flawed business models. It's ironic that so many smart businesspeople bet their careers on companies without doing the kind of due diligence research they would apply to a simple stock pick. But capital was easy to find, big salaries and bigger stock options were in the air. Blinded by the e-commerce hype, a lot of people afraid of missing the gravy train proceeded to ignore the fundamental principle of capitalism: it's about making money. The promise of the dot-coms relied on the faulty premise that a brand, or "traffic," or even mere revenues—and not profit—could turn a Web site into the NBC of the Internet. Everyone rushed into what was essentially a massive pyramid scheme: the first ones in made money and the last ones in got hosed. (After five years in business, the management at Amazon.com, virtually the only dot-com left standing, has just changed its slogan from "Get big fast" to "March to profitability"— and that's after having lost $1.4 billion, so far.) Here's what those young dot-commies should have done to get a rational evaluation of what a company's prospects really were:

1. Find out who's in the deal. That's the primary question head-hunters and investors ask about start-ups. Who is the founder? What kind of board have they put together? What VC firm and investment bank is involved in the financing? How impressive is the management team?

2. Look for conflicts on the board and mixed agendas. The bigger the job you are taking, the more clued in you want to be to the problems. What are they? Can they be fixed?

3. Evaluate the fundamentals. Being on the edge with a new idea is certainly important for a start-up or a relatively new company. But if you are looking to score some early successes in your career, you want to be with a company that has a genuine opportunity to make some money.

4. Try to get a sense of the culture of the company. How much turnover is there among managers and top talent? Find out how tough decisions get made. Do they get rid of poor performers? Who is the top talent hired recently? One quick way inside is to talk to a few people who have left.

5. Spend enough time with the person hiring you to get a sense of who he really is and how representative of the company he might be. If you don't like him or his take on the business, will you like your new colleagues?

6. Talk to customers and find out what they think of the company.

7. Talk to competitors.

8. Be prepared for each conversation. Work hard on coming up with thoughtful, incisive questions. That will require doing some research on the company and its management. The public information about a start-up will obviously be limited. But you can check out the top management, find out where they were before, what kind of experience they have, whether they moved up or side-

ways to join this particular start-up. Early-stage companies are likely to have more of a paper trail, with company Web sites offering free access to bios of the top officers as well as recent press releases and news stories about what the company is up to.

9. If you're in business school, your teachers or recent graduates may know something about the firm or management. Ask them. They'll be impressed.

### Evaluating a Turnaround

Getting positioned in a well-known company that is about to make a comeback can be a real career maker for a young manager. The company's new success will radiate to those who were on the team when it happened. In 1991, recruiters were not much impressed by IBM managers who helped tarnish one of the greatest brands in business history. When Lew Gerstner took over in 1992, IBM was essentially in a turnaround situation. Any young manager who joined Gerstner's company would have played a role in one of the most impressive comebacks in U.S. business history—not a bad thing to have on your résumé today. Riding a successful turnaround back up the Dow or NASDAQ is also a quick way to make some money. The people who helped Continental Airlines and Texas Instruments regain their former glory did very well indeed. Many of the same criteria for checking a start-up apply to companies trying to make a comeback:

1. Who's in the deal? Again, you want to be clear about who the top management is and how decisions will get made. Leadership is particularly crucial in a turnaround. Lee Iacocca brought Chrysler back from the dead, and Continental's Gordon Bethune proved

what a difference one person could make with what he himself called "a lousy airline." Find out as much as you can about the new CEO. Typically, a company will try to bring in someone who has already proved that he can revive a company. Turnaround CEOs comprise a small and exclusive club. If the company you're looking at has a known turnaround expert at the helm, taking a job there could be a career maker. If the new boss is a question mark, you should look elsewhere. When the Lucent board fired CEO Richard McGinn in 2000, no one was surprised. The surprise came when they replaced McGinn with Henry Schacht, Lucent's original CEO, who had retired and handed the company over to McGinn. Critics wondered how Schacht could fix Lucent's problems, many of which McGinn had inherited from Schacht. Finding top people to go to the struggling Lucent is a challenge.

2. Get on the Internet and find as many articles as you can about the company, particularly on the subject of what went wrong. Talk to people who used to work there about the problems that caused the company's decline, and then ask in your interview what the company has been doing to fix those problems. Showing that you've been thinking about the company's problems even before you've been hired is bound to impress your interviewer. Some innovative suggestions about what might be done would clinch the job.

3. Who are the top people hired recently? You do not necessarily want to be the first person brought in. Turnarounds are tough; they need the most talent possible, and for you to succeed, you will need to be part of a talented team. Make sure some other smart people have done their due diligence.

## SURPRISE THEM

Remember: hiring managers interview job candidates for a living. Your challenge is to wake them up and prove that you're the best person to have entered their office in ages. When I interview job candidates, I am always looking to be surprised. There are a lot of competent people out there, but the exceptional executives are always a bit different. They surprise you in some way—with their brains, energy, humor, ideas, leadership potential, or humility. Sometimes all it takes is asking the right question, or, better still, the right question that no one else has asked. There's nothing like the delight you experience when you ask a question and the other person's head snaps back in awe. The ability to surprise is one of the most effective traits managers can display. Do it all the time and you will never be an anonymous employee. Surprise your boss, your colleagues, your people, your customers, with your work ethic, with your results, with interesting ways of doing things, innovations, importing new ideas from other companies. (Surprising people with *bad* news, however, is to be avoided. Let them know when a problem is coming. Solicit people's help early when you see problems coming. One good reason to bring in other people to help you is that when a project does not work out, it will not be solely your failure.)

A good beginning for the surprising career can be that first phone call for an interview. Everybody else is sending résumés with cover letters or e-mails. I get about twenty e-mails a day from experienced executives looking for jobs. The most promising résumés we circulate around the office, but they will never be our highest priority. We're looking to recruit people who are not interested in being recruited. A well-executed, old-fashioned phone call, however, is more likely to catch our attention. In fact, a series of phone calls will show your persistence. I have often found in my career that a headhunter can be most successful operating after everyone else has gone home for the day. I have found that most people give up at the same time; if you continue working, that is when the magic can happen. When I started calling around to search firms for my first job twenty years ago, I had my little spiel about who I was, why I was eager to work in the search business, and what I thought I could offer. I talked a lot to administrative assistants, and never underestimated how helpful they could be in getting me on the phone with their boss. To get them on my side, I was always courteous and respectful. But I was also persistent in my efforts to get to the hiring manager. One of the tricks I learned early on was that if you call executives at the office early in the morning or late in the day, after six P.M., for instance, they are more likely to pick up their own phone. I was never shy about asking for an interview, and more times than not I got one.

## PREPARE YOUR PITCH

One of the worst things you can say, on the phone or during a face-to-face interview, is, "Hmm, that's an interesting question," and then spend time thinking about your answer. Frankly, interviewers, as we have seen, tend to ask the obvious questions—"Tell me about your strengths, weaknesses, how you fixed a problem"—and if you do not have a good answer, the hiring managers will immediately rate you as a no-talent. Not only should you have your stories ready, you should work on them. Practice your pitch on friends, colleagues, your wife, husband, the plumber. Anyone who has a favorite anecdote or joke knows that the more you tell it, the better you get at telling it. You will be asked, "What have you done?" and you should be ready with the answer, including plenty of details and an account of the mechanisms that you used to make things happen. I usually ask that same question when interviewing candidates, and I never cease to be amazed when allegedly experienced managers seem to be stymied by it, or lack passion in describing their accomplishments. If you have not achieved anything that you are excited to talk about, then you better ask yourself why—and get to work.

Before I make a call, before I make a presentation, and certainly before I go into a shoot-out with other search firms to win an assignment, I do as much research as possible about the company, the industry, and the best people for the position, whether they're looking for a job or not. I pride myself on my careful research and always have a plan. As informed as I am about a company, I only ask questions. A CEO is not looking for a lecture about his own company or an industry he knows better than any headhunter. And, of course, I try to surprise the company with better questions than my competition. I recommend having several questions ready to go—written down, so that under pressure you do not forget them. About fifteen years ago, I switched from writing my questions on a yellow pad to using a bound composition book that has a built-in cloth bookmark. I keep notes from my research in these composition books, and in the margins I write two or three important questions for each session, typically probing the marketplace and the company's strategies for gaining a bigger share of it: What are the company's biggest concerns or problems? Who is their main competition—the company that can really knock them out of the game? Your interviewer is likely to be impressed that you are anticipating problems. Every company is looking for problem solvers. The more insightful and unusual the questions you come up with the better.

Make sure that your interview is not full of excuses about what you were doing before you started looking for a job. Great leaders do not indulge in excuses because they find ways to avoid failure and to come up with innovative solutions to problems that mystified other managers. Sometimes turning a failure into a success means getting to the right person and warning him that failure is around the corner so it is now time to end the project or exit the deal or that business. Be self-confident enough to share the praise. If you've had a previous job, try to get the subject around to how you've worked with colleagues. Make it clear that you're a team player. When I pre-interview candidates for my clients, I listen carefully for the word "we."

The other thing I learned early on and recommend to job seekers is that once the interview is over ask the interviewer for some feedback: "What are your concerns?" "What did I leave out?" "What would have made it a better interview?" You will be doing job interviews throughout your career. Why not get better every time? The interviewer is bound to be impressed by the work you're putting into this meeting. The information you get will also help you to close the interview and to know what to say in a follow-up letter. If they have a specific concern about you, perhaps there is a name you can give them, a person they might call who will assuage that concern. I found that by being well prepared, asking good questions, and then, after the interview, requesting feedback, I got hiring managers who would have not been inclined to spend much time with an inexperienced twenty-three-year-old to take me seriously.

## PLAY TO YOUR STRENGTHS

If you already have a job, make it clear that you're looking for bigger challenges: "I want to leverage my skills at building sales organizations." Or creating new products. Or dealing with customer service. Or executing business strategies. Whatever your expertise is, press that advantage. Explain what you've accomplished in your current job, particularly what had the most impact. "I love making things happen, building things, growing things." Every time you make a career move, people will ask you what you did. I myself like to ask job candidates what they did in their last three jobs that they think was most meaningful, and what I really have in mind is things that they did that no one else could have done. I want to know what obstacles they ran into, how they sidestepped them. From a manager, I want to hear how they focused on the problem, got other people engaged in a solution, pulled the right team together, aimed them in the right direction so that costs were cut, profits were increased. I want to hear a story about how you made a difference. And I am looking for plenty of details that prove you were really there.

## HOW TO FIND A NEW JOB—FAST

Headhunters get tons of e-mails every day from job seekers. Most of them put me to sleep. They all seem to begin in the same way: "I am a proven executive. . . ." Would anyone claim to be "a green" or "failed" executive? Those who escape the cliché opener tend to go for something cute or downright weird. When you are looking for a job, you have 30 to 60 seconds to grab them, no matter the form of communication. You must get to the point: Why they should hire you?

They are looking for managers who make things happen. You must begin immediately by stating what you have made happen at your current company: "In my current position of sales manager at XYZ Corporation, I turned around this sales organization and got the following results. . . . Or, you put the right team together on the right project and got a new solution; you got a new customer to buy from your company that they had been trying to get for years, and so on. Results, results. Of course, other job seekers will be vying for their attention. There are three things you can do to beat your competition:

1. Find the right company and get to the right person. Your research should be focused on identifying the companies most likely to hire you because they need someone with your expertise or are just doing a lot of hiring. Once you have a shortlist, call everyone you know and ask them if they know anyone in the company who might have advice about the best person to talk to. And then get on the phone and do everything to get your foot in the door for a face-to-face interview. The old-fashioned personal call, as I have already stressed, is the way to go these days. Don't let an assistant get in your way; keep calling ("All I need is five minutes with your boss.") until they give in. Keep phoning as many hiring managers as you can—ten to twelve calls a day. Don't forget trying to call at odd hours, early or late in the day, when you might actually get the boss on the phone.

2. Be prepared—and be surprising. Your time is limited, so hit them with what you've done, and what you know you can do for

their company. When selling yourself, always be brief and to the point. Prove you're a well-prepared, smart, no-nonsense person from the get-go. But no matter how impressive your pitch might be, the person on the other end of the phone will soon be looking for a way to sign off. Raise some specific questions—the kind a smart headhunter asks a client: What keeps you up at night? If you could find a star performer, where would you put her in the organization? Of all the people you've ever hired, who was the best and what made them so? What is your organization's biggest challenge today? And never let them hang up without scheduling a meeting. In fact, don't ask, set the time: "Let's get together for an early breakfast. I promise it will be worth your while." I cannot tell you how many times clients have told our firm we got hired because "you asked the best questions."

3. Be confident. You must convince them that they need you. Often people give up too soon or do not put enough time into their plan and questions. Attitude is key: You are the person who will make a difference. Everything you say and how you say it should convey your self-confidence. You can even transform a "we are not hiring" into an opportunity: "We're both in the same industry, and, frankly, I plan on landing a big job in the next sixty days or so. We probably ought to get to know each other." Point out that chances are you might be working for the competition or even be a potential customer. You have nothing to lose, and the upside is that they might decide that they can spare the time to meet this impressive person at the other end of the phone.

What if you do not have a great example of something you did in your current job to make a difference, or you have messed up your career and therefore have a big problem in the eyes of people who do the hiring? If this is the case, there are things you can do to increase your talent quotient.

## LEARN HOW TO BE TALENTED—AND WORK AT IT

I cannot teach you to be a brilliant corporate visionary or to be a creative thinker. But there are all sorts of things that you can learn so that when recruiters look at your résumé and meet you, they will mark you down on their shortlist. The kinds of people that frustrate me the most are those who are forever finding excuses outside themselves for why things aren't working. One of my standard questions in job interviews is to ask candidates to think back two years about the specific things they wanted to do better as a leader or manager and tell me how they measure up today against those goals. "I'm currently pretty much who I want to be and doing what I want to do"—is not the answer I'm looking for, though I hear it surprisingly often. What I want to hear is, "I wanted to get better at financial analysis and at pulling the trigger faster on poor performers." Know where your weaknesses lie, and improve them.

People who think they have nothing more to learn will never qualify as talent. They either have no clue about their weaknesses, a dangerous prospect, or they lack humility, a warning sign of a manager who is not likely to want anyone around challenging him, no matter how talented. In today's world, where new information rains on us daily and the exponential advances of technology challenge even the fastest minds in business, no one can stop learning. Over the years, I have noted that the most exceptional leaders I have met are perpetual students of their industries. There is a reason General Electric trumpets itself as a "Global Learning Company" in its annual reports and is not ashamed to brag about what the company has learned from Toyota ("asset management") and Allied Signal ("Six Sigma"). GE is not embarrassed by the fact that Trilogy, Cisco, and Oracle have helped digitize their company. Great organizations are eager to educate their employees in "early-career programs" in financial management, engineering, manufacturing, and other areas. For their best performers they have "advanced management training" programs. Spreading knowledge around companies has become so important in today's Talent Economy that recruiters at my firm have identified "chief learning officer"—the individual who keeps new information and knowledge flowing through a company—as a hot new career opportunity even in a down economy.

For me, the "Formula Five"—honesty and integrity, intellectual firepower, energy and passion, leadership, humility—is the gold standard for talent. But these are all *personal* skills, and we can get better at each of them. Here's how you can work on improving your "Formula Five" traits:

**Honesty and Integrity** Often in business, we run into situations where compromising our values will put money in our pockets. The best leaders resist the temptation without a thought. Nothing will derail a career faster than the whiff of scandal. At the outset of your career, you must make a commitment to ethical business practices. "You can trust him; he's solid." If people can say that about you, it's amazing how many other things they can forget. Conducting business according to a strict sense of what's right (and wrong) is something that anyone can decide to do. It is a matter of *character,* and people change all the time for the better. It is also about *values,* and in the business world every manager—and company—has to be clear about priorities. Most companies now have institutionalized "mission statements" that lay out what the organization's main principles are. Every manager ought to have his own personal mission statement to refer to.

**Intellectual Firepower** You may not have the highest IQ in the game, but you can certainly learn more. I have interviewed many top executives who were far from brilliant, but they were successful, mainly because they learned what they had to know—and hired the best people to back them up in their weak areas. In a lifetime as an autodidact, I have noticed that there are several areas in which I know more than some of my smartest friends and colleagues. All it takes is some focused reading or spending time with experts in the field. To rise in business, you have to keep learning.

**Energy and Passion** The moment you don't feel like doing something, do something. To survive in a big job, never mind succeed, you have to be able to do several things at once. Work on your execution skills. Each quarter pick a couple of the things that are crucial to your job and learn to do them better. And faster. To save time, make quicker phone calls; write shorter e-mails; focus your meetings. Ask better questions. In whatever you do, there are always a few things that are critical. Know what they are and make sure they get done first. Find out what is critical to other people getting their jobs done and apply yourself to improving performance all around. And work hard. That, however, does not always mean longer hours. Figure out when you work most efficiently. I am an owl. I like to work late at night and into the early hours. Inexperienced managers are likely to have trouble managing their time. Evaluate your productivity. Looking back on my own career, I have noticed that most of my successes have come near the end of my efforts, rarely at the beginning. People talk about the "80/20 rule"—you get all your results from 20 percent of your activity. I agree with that, but I would add that the 20 percent does not materialize unless you go all the way. If you give 80 percent, you do not get results. The magic happens on the *last* 20 percent.

**Leadership** Everyone can improve in this area. The best way is to attach yourself to an exceptional leader. Leaders take the time to communicate their vision and bring everyone into the project. Put yourself in the other person's shoes by asking questions like, "If I had to do this job or pull off that project, what would help me get excited about it? What would I want a leader to do for me?" The best leaders, as I have tried to show, develop pretty much the same leadership model: they engage their organizations in their vision, which they develop by listening to their people and customers. You have to become more than a "slogan leader" who excels only at describing the vision; the exceptional leader is also able to guide people toward achieving the company's goals. Crucial, too, is making sure everyone is absolutely clear about their roles in this process— and then get out of their way and let them do their jobs. The final step is to hold people accountable. That is basically how great leaders operate, and it is a model that anyone can imitate.

**Humility** The more exceptional leaders I interview and work with, the higher I have come to rate humility as a personality requirement for business success. Humble executives know what they do not know and therefore are learning all the time. The best leaders are learners—and they create learning environments. They are able to share credit because their self-esteem does not come from winning praise but from getting things done. Every time you find yourself about to take credit for something, consider how you can spread the praise around. Every time you think you know your job cold, find something new to learn. Every time you have a big win, go to your colleagues and thank them for their help.

## MAKING THINGS HAPPEN

To build the kind of career that will label you as talent, never stop thinking about how to make things happen and never let your superiors forget how much you are contributing to their success. You must turn yourself into a certain kind of person. Every day you must ask yourself:

- What am I doing that my boss or his peers or my boss's boss is going to notice?
- What am I doing today that's going to make a difference the next time I'm talking to a hiring manager?

If you can't seem to make anything happen, it might be the company you're working for. But if colleagues at your level are succeeding and you're not, then you are the problem. Do not, however, beat yourself up over this. Be delighted that you've recognized that you've got a problem and that because you're young you have time to fix it. You are probably making one of these common mistakes:

- Doing or saying the wrong things. For example: if you're in sales, your technique may be wrong or off. You need to become a better salesperson. This can be learned.

- Interacting with the wrong people. It is difficult to achieve the right goals with the wrong people. Often young managers get stymied only because they do not have the right people around them. Sales or marketing people are out there in the field killing themselves, but nothing is happening because they are talking to the wrong people.

If you think you are working flat out but are still running in place, here are some suggestions for getting things moving:

- Be bold. Ask for things. Ask to talk to people. "I'd like to explain why I should be your next VP of marketing." Always take the initiative. Do not be afraid to shock people. It's one way to be recognized, and you will not get your superiors' attention without trying to do some things differently. Years ago, I was interviewing someone for a job at my own firm. I had no intention of hiring him; he did not have the kind of background that we were looking for at that stage in the company's growth; he was also physically unkempt. Frankly, I felt sorry for the guy, and perhaps to assuage my own guilt at the end of the interview I said, "Let me show you around the office." "That'd be great," he replied. "I'd like to see where I'm going to sit." I hired him, and he turned out to be one of the brightest people we ever hired, our first researcher, and a huge asset to the company. He surprised me. It works.
- Be innovative. Sponsor things that are new and different in your company. Initiate conferences and meetings.
- Research your organization's problems. And then start figuring out how to solve them. One of the main marks of talent is being

a problem solver. Find out what other successful companies are doing and figure out how to adapt those ideas to your situation. Companies all around the world have benefited from Wal-Mart's inventory innovations and Motorola's experiments in quality control. You don't have to invent the wheel to get credit for getting things rolling in your own organization. Import new ideas and information from other companies.

- Volunteer for tough new projects. To stand out you have to be on hand for the big successes in your organization. To get the reputation as a problem solver, you have to go where the problems are.

## THE ULTIMATE SECRET: RELATIONSHIPS

If I had to sum up in one word what it takes to build a successful career it would be "relationships." Great careers are built on relationships—with clients and customers, to be sure, but also with the people you work with, your peers as well as your bosses. If you value talent, if your surround yourself with talented people at every stage of your career, you cannot help but be successful. You need to know who the best performers are in your company and in the industry at large. You must imitate and learn from them. For someone starting out, you must find the best people in your company at your same age group or job level—the consensus A players. Seek them out, become their friends and colleagues. Invite them to lunch, take them to dinner or a sporting event, and talk to them candidly. "Everything seems to be going right for you," is one way to approach them. "How do you make it happen?" Ask for criticism: "What am I doing wrong?" "What do I need to learn?"

Listen to what they say. These are the people who are going places—and should you become part of their team, they might even take you along. When John Chambers left Wang for a top job at Cisco, several colleagues followed. Groups of people from Xerox went to Apple and Microsoft, and then from Apple to Dell and Compaq. People who get big jobs always like to bring along someone they know and trust. Why not be one of them? Even if they do not invite you immediately, give them a call. Or if someone you respect who is a couple of levels above you at your company is leaving, call him. Congratulate him on his new job; say that you're sorry to see him leave but you were wondering whether you might be able to get some advice about managing your own career. Maybe he'll confide in you that he's looking to hire new people.

I know it might strike you as a bit aggressive or pushy. But in the business world, no one gets ahead without at least aiming in the forward direction. Sure, you might get rejected. But take it from a headhunter who has spent decades calling talented people on the phone and having them—or, worse, their administrative assistants—say "no way." If you're worried about getting your feelings hurt, you will have trouble launching a big career.

Building a network of relationships is something you must start early in your career and never stop expanding. This network will become part of who you are and how you move up in your career. No headhunter can operate without such a list of contacts, and no business leader can thrive without a network, either. Creating the right kind of business network and networking your network is an art form.

## CHAPTER 8

*You're Always Your Own Headhunter:*

*Growing Your Talent Network*

Back in my first search job at R.F. Timbers, when I decided that robotics would be the secret to my success, I did not know one person in the field. But my boss Dick Timbers had a contact at a company that published manufacturing documents who got me a list of every company in the country that was manufacturing robotics or using them. I went through that list and transferred the names to index cards categorized "RMs" and "AMs"—for robotics manufacturers and automation manufacturers—and "RUs" and "AUs"—for robotics users and automation users. I figured if I got to each one of these people, I would have something that no one else had—a connection to all the players in a new industry. I created a brochure promoting our firm's expertise in the field, began calling around, and soon realized that there were a lot of companies with jobs to fill. It turned out I was the first search firm to call them; better still, I seemed actually to know something about their industry. I thus quickly created an identity in the marketplace. Of course, the Age of Robotics did not happen. But our work with these automation companies led us into the computer field and other high-tech markets, which became the foundation of our search firm's success. In the course of scrambling for an expertise that would give me an edge on my colleagues and competitors, I had created my first talent network.

A headhunter is only as good as the names in his Palm Pilot. If I don't know how to create a network of talented people and use it on behalf of demanding clients, then I'm in the wrong business. In fact, if I don't make finding talent my highest priority, *I'm out of business.* Christian & Timbers now has an extensive database of hundreds of thousands of names, including potential job candidates as well as reliable talent scouts in every industry we service. My personal talent network is probably close to a thousand people, and I am always asking for new recommendations. I am not shy about calling people like Steve Jobs, Carly Fiorina, John Chambers, or VCs like John Doerr or Vinod Khosla for advice or suggestions about a current recruiting assignment, and they will call me. We are part of one another's talent networks. In the early stages of the Hewlett-Packard CEO search, for example, I called Scott McNealy at Sun Microsystems for some names. He called me back with some suggestions (including the suggestion that I not try to recruit one of his top people). As headhunter I do not merely depend on my talent network, I *am* my talent network.

And so are you. If business success today depends on talent, as I have been arguing in this book, and if having talent makes yours the kind of organization where new talent wants to work, then you must have your own network. In fact, every manager in your company who hires people better have his own talent network. Smart CEOs and the best general managers do not just have information about markets, technology, competition, or globalization; they also make it their job to have intelligence on talent. They know that their talent network is not just their reservoir of talent but also a pipeline for funding, sales, new ideas, and reliable advice when they need it. In fact, at every stage of your career, it will be your business network that drives your success. And you take your talent network with you wherever you go.

It is never too late to start building a list of connections or to renew the network you already have. The earlier you can start building a talent network, however, the sooner you will benefit from it. Success in business, as I have stressed, is mainly about relationships. How can you build a career or your company without exposing yourself to every opportunity possible? There are people out there you do not even know who can change your career. You must meet them.

### The Earlier the Better

For young people, that means right now, whether you are in college, business school, or your first job. Talent is the tide that you can ride to the top. Start getting those people on your side now. When the young Bill Gates was launching his company with a workforce so small you could count it on your fingers, he knew he needed two things fast—more talented people and more new ideas. He wrangled a visit to Xerox's Palo Alto Research Center and checked out what the local wizards were up to. And then kept in touch. Gates soon lured away many of the PARC's best people to the young Microsoft. Steve Jobs recruited others for Apple.

If you're still in school, make sure you get to know the people in your classes who stand out, who seem to know what they're doing, the winners. Stay in touch. Once you land your first job, immediately begin identifying the talented people among your colleagues; figure out who your possible mentors might be—and get to know them. The one thing I would try to teach every manager, from an up-and-coming director of marketing or a VP of engineering to a CEO is this: find out who the best people are and then spend time with them. If you're in a junior management position, you certainly want to associate yourself with a boss who is a winner. Consider how many people rise in the world of business (and politics) on the coattails of an extraordinarily talented manger. Mentors are an essential variable in a successful career. Ask them questions, try to learn what they've already learned. And, as you move on to other companies, keep in touch. They're the foundation of your growing talent network. Believe me: people who've worked closely with Lou Gerstner or Jack Welch or John Chambers or Steve Jobs or Michael Eisner give them a call when they need some advice. Exceptional leaders enjoy schmoozing about talent with headhunters and VCs. The more important the project, the quicker you will get a callback. The best leaders are natural talent scouts who cannot bear thinking that there may be some gifted managers out there they have not heard about. We routinely lose leading candidates during the reference-checking process. But such setbacks only underline how important an ever expanding talent pipeline is in a Talent Economy.

### Ask Everyone You Know About Prospective Talent

Ask *everyone*—including family, friends, college acquaintances, prominent alumni of your schools, and ex-bosses. These are the people you know best and who know you and your business. There's no reason to be shy. A friend or a friend of a friend is an easy and productive place to begin creating a talent network.

I am always eager to discover a new name to add to my network. During interviews, I routinely ask people who they think are the best in their industry. Whenever you're talking to someone in your business or in areas related to what you do, you should always inquire about talent. Dealing with customers is a perfect opportunity to pick up some intelligence. "Who's the best salesman out there calling on you?" You definitely want to know the name of that person. And then talk to him. Managers are constantly doing market research about products and technology; they have to know what is in the pipeline. Do your market research on talent. "Is there a general manager out there who is better than I am, more aggressive?" "Who's the best CIO, the one who really has great ideas for serving his customers?"

You don't have to begin by calling Steve Jobs or John Chambers. Take advantage of the network that's already within reach. As I was writing this section, my father came up with a great candidate for my own company, a woman from one of our competitors whom we ended up recruiting. Dad may be seventy-eight, but he's still in the employment business and has been a prime resource in my talent network since my first job.

### Everyone Already Has at Least a Mini–Talent Network

Use your existing relationships to create new relationships. I started with my father. If you give it a moment's thought, I bet you'll come up with well-connected business sources in your immediate circle. You know that parlor game "Six Degrees of Kevin Bacon"—where you take a name and see how quickly you can connect that name through friends, associates, family, other actors, and movies to the actor Kevin Bacon? You can play a similar game with business connections for fun and profit.

Exponential math is extremely important to networking talent. Write down the names of ten people you could call for referrals of possible candidates you might consider. Ask every person you call for three or more names. Next time you have a job to fill, you will already have a list of thirty or more people to call. I have a young associate in New York, Jeff Shapiro, who works closely with me on all my searches. His first job in the search business was for a solo practitioner. "She'd give me a search along with ten or twelve names, and my job was to generate bigger lists," recalls Jeff, who later worked for Egon Zehnder, one of the biggest search firms in the world. "When you don't work for a big firm, you have to get extremely good at finding people and building your talent network." The tools are all out there. It just depends on how ambitious and serious you are about finding talent. My rule of thumb is: they are all getable.

The bigger the job, the more access you will have to the players in your industry. Soon after Jeff came to work for me, he got involved in a search I was doing with Kleiner, Perkins for the CEO of Firedrop.com, a new Internet communications company that Vinod Khosla had invested in (along with Internet guru Esther

Dyson and Bill Joy, who, along with Khosla, is a cofounder of Sun Microsystems). With such an important position in play, Kleiner, Perkins at our side, and such Internet pioneers already involved, Jeff was able to reach Mike Homer, one of the founders of Netscape. "I actually had several conversations with Mike, and over an accumulated couple of hours on the phone, he was feeding me names, companies to check out, other people to source," recalls Shapiro, still amazed. Obviously, it was a thrill for Jeff to spend so much time talking to a Silicon Valley legend. But he also was expanding his talent network. "Hi, Mike Homer suggested I give you a call . . ." is going to open some doors. Even if those people aren't interested in that particular job, they will be available next time around, at least for another conversation or as a new talent resource.

What you think may be a tiny talent network could thus quickly expand into something much more impressive. The best-connected people in your industry—and in the world—all started with a small network.

*Making the Call*

Cold calls to anyone are not easy, never mind calling important people in your industry who have never heard of you. But if you keep one thing in mind, picking up the phone will be a lot easier: essentially, you are asking someone to help you, and most people like to help. The key is to leave the kind of message that will increase your odds of a callback. Be specific, and appeal to their needs and interests. If you're trying to launch or grow a small company, make a list of the important people in the industry. Call them up and leave a message: "I need help filling a top management position." Almost anyone will be interested, either out of curiosity about your new company or because they're looking for a board seat. They'll call back, and you've broken the ice, you get to talk, maybe have a meeting. And if during the conversation you bring up some of the challenges you're facing and he's offered some advice, you're already on the way to getting this new member of your network to play an advisory role in your company.

If it is a particular position you are trying to fill, you can leave a message explicitly seeking advice: "I need some help on a project I'm working on." And then state the area—streaming video, for example, optical networking, currency fluctuations, whatever your area of expertise. At the other end, he's thinking he doesn't know who you are, but he needs to expand his own network. So he returns your call. People who are good at things enjoy proving it. Most people like to give advice.

As eager as you are to add these new people to your network, keep in mind that as you talk, they will also be gauging your intelligence and overall worthiness to be in their network. More important, good questions will get them talking. The better the conversation, the more likely they will remember you.

### The Key (Again) Is Research

Headhunters know that the foundation of any search is how much intelligence you can put together on who the talent is and where they work. And I'm not talking about the obvious talent. Your competitors are already onto them. To find the up-and-comers or the diamonds in the rough, you have to get creative. My company employs researchers who stay on top of what is happening in specific industries. But we also expect those partners and associates responsible for covering an industry to know where the talent is. We are constantly alerting each other with tips on talent. Their networks become the firm's networks. But the key to finding the not-so-obvious talent, the people about to begin their career trajectories, is to dig and call around.

## Keep an Eye Out for the Winners Inside Your Own Organization

The basis for a very good network may already exist inside your own company. Connect with it, build it, shape it. The people who are going to make your career may already be working with you or for you. They're generally those who get promoted the fastest, particularly in large corporations. When I do reference checks on real talent, the next hot CEOs, what I hear people saying about them is, "Rick's the guy that everyone wants to work with. There's no turnover in his organization." Or: "Mary is the person we turn to when we have a department or division that is in trouble."

Those are the people you ought to be recruiting into your own network because someday, down the line, Rick or Mary might be exactly the person you need to talk to for advice or about a job offer. Many of the managers I talk to are so focused on external goals, so obsessed about making their numbers, that they fail to recognize the value of their own people and what makes them succeed. Jack Welch looked at it from the other side: GE's success was a result of the kind of talent he hired. Welch's goal for years was to be number one and two in every market GE is in. But what made that possible is another goal he set for GE: get the *best* people in *every* job. The way to start is to make sure the best managers you have are in the right jobs and getting the promotions they deserve, and begin building talented teams around them.

### Your Network Includes Your Direct Reports

If you are not building a talent network out of the people who report to you today, you are on the verge of losing whatever power
you have gained. The people under you should know who you are
and what you care about most. You should also know them and
their career goals. How can you benefit from talent when you don't
even know when it's staring you in the face? You want all the people capable of making you look good in your network. Jack Welch
deserves all the praise he gets. But by focusing on Welch's success,
the media too often ignores the fact that one of the keys to his astonishing twenty-year run at General Electric was the quality of his
direct reports, people who are now running such major organizations as Intuit, Primedia, Conseco, 3M, and Home Depot. I don't
care how good Welch was; he would be less than Jack Welch without the talent he cultivated around himself.

### Pay Attention to What Is Happening Outside Your Company

After a recent talk I gave, someone asked, "What if you can't afford
the best people?" My answer was that you have to find the superstars of the future before the headhunters are on to them and early
enough in their career trajectories so that you can afford them.
Most managers know when the competition is eating their lunch.
But do you know who is responsible for the strategy that is killing
you? You should have that manager on your side—before her boss
figures out she's a star. While the competition is waiting for young
managers to make their mark, you should be looking for those innate leadership skills that are evidence that it's only a matter of
time before they score big. They may only be a regional director

today, but you know they have the talent to be a CEO. Grab them now, while they're cheap.

### Even People Who Turn You Down Can Be Part of Your Talent Network

When candidates say they're not interested in talking about a new position, keep them talking. Make a point, engage them in a conversation, ask a question: "I understand why you're not interested, but what would it take for you to consider leaving your current position?" "Do you have any suggestions for other people to call?" "If you had to fill this job, whom would you ask?" Notice how such questions transform them from job candidates into sources for other potential job candidates. One of my associates was trying to get the head of marketing at E-Trade interested in a job we were trying to fill. Before they got very far, E-Trade's CEO got wind of it and offered him the job of president, which he happily grabbed. But we're still in touch. After all, he might need a search firm one of these days, and we might come with a job he finds attractive. Most important, there's a relationship between him and Christian & Timbers. He is now part of our talent network.

### Be Persistent

Headhunters have to develop the skin of a rhino. To create an effective talent network, you, too, will have to get used to rejection. I am convinced that one of the keys to my own success is that I never give up. Even when I want to give up, I make another phone call. And you must not be afraid to call people when they do not want to be called—at home, for example. Several years ago, I recall, I was trying to get through to an excellent general manager at Borland Software. At the time, Borland was a hot software company, and there weren't many excellent software general managers in the Bay Area. I must have called his office twenty times. His secretary had clearly been warned not to put through any calls from headhunters. I had a home number for him from a previous conversation, but it had been disconnected, and now he wasn't listed. Figuring he may have moved, I began calling information in the six or so regional calling areas within commuting distance of Silicon Valley. Unfortunately, his name was not all that unusual, and I got a listing or two in every area. I would call the number, ask whoever answered if this was the home of the Borland general manager. I did this one or two evenings a week for several weeks in vain—and then I reached him. Just plain luck. He had recently relisted his phone number. I had made about a hundred calls in total before I heard his voice. (I wish I could say that this all-out telephone effort ended in recruiting him for a client, but it didn't.)

### Be Aggressive

When you see, hear, or meet someone at an industry event who impresses you, introduce yourself. In fact, don't be afraid to knock over several people to get to that person. We are all susceptible to flattery. Everyone with something to say wants confirmation that someone is listening. Give her your card, ask her if you might get together. If you think that person ought to be working for you, you will have to put yourself in a position to make her an offer.

"But I don't want to seem pushy," people tell me. You would not believe how "pushy" a good headhunter has to be. I know head-hunters who, when they haven't been able to get a potential candi-date to return their calls, show up on that person's doorstep, demanding to know why the guy won't talk to them. Personally, I have never gone that far, because I think it's a waste of time, maybe even counterproductive. But colleagues of mine swear that when they confront a recalcitrant potential candidate with their own ex-citement and passion for the assignment, if they can convey that the job is an opportunity of a lifetime, people do listen. I know of a case where a venture capitalist heard through his network about a Compaq executive who might be right to run one of the Internet start-ups he was funding. The VC proceeded to arrange for his tar-get to be invited to speak at a conference his firm was sponsoring at Duke University and then to play golf later in his foursome. During the round, he pitched the upside potential of his start-ups, and before the guy from Compaq was in the shower, the VC had him thinking about running one of his companies. It was a total setup. Was that pushy or aggressive? It may have even been a bit on the devious side. But the strategy worked. The man from Compaq eventually signed on as CEO of one of that VC's companies.

### Try Not to Be a Total Jerk

Networking, after all, is about developing contacts, discovering new resources, and making friends. You want people to want to help you, and that is not likely to happen if you're inclined to be a stone in social situations or enjoy wielding a hammer as a man-ager. Headhunters know that sometimes the best people to have in your network are top corporate administrative assistants. Who better to help you get an appointment with a hotly recruited manager or get him on the phone? So—in the course of doing business, be nice to the gatekeepers, because you never know when you'll want to get back through that gate.

### Never Miss an Opportunity to Get a New Name

I ask these questions all the time of people I'm interviewing: "Whom do you most admire in your organization?" "Who do you think is the best leader in the company you're working for? Why?" I also ask candidates who they think the most talented people in their industry are and what they admire most about them. From their answers I get not only a good sense of what this person thinks is important in a manager, I also get some new names to research.

You can do the same with people you've just hired. All of us tend to get locked into the concerns of our own businesses. We get sheltered from what's happening outside. Incoming talent is likely to have a better sense of what's going on in the industry; they may be more clued in to the rising stars in their classes or age groups. They might even have worked at two or more companies during the time you've been at one. New hires, if they really are talented, are bound to have their own talent networks. Better still, they will be eager to please. When I hire people for my own firm, I'm also hiring their talent networks—and that includes their friends, relatives, and partners. I met the boyfriend of our first manager of research at a company outing, was impressed, and ended up hiring him. He now runs our semiconductor and electronics practice. Make sure your HR department and everyone else on your interviewing team is trained to ask candidates and new employees about other people they might talk to about jobs at your company.

### Include Competitors in Your Talent Network

"Strategic relationship" has become an overused concept, but it's still a phrase that will get a competitor to pick up the phone. You can begin any conversation with the possibility of working together on a project or simply asking for an opinion about a common problem you're up against. The best venture capitalists are always having lunch and dinner with one another, talking about their deals and the talent they need to make them go. That's their business. And while most corporate types are not likely to be spending as much time with the competition as VCs do, sharing data or information with other people in your industry is a good habit to get into. It also provides an opportunity to get to know new people in the industry—and add them to your talent network.

### Every Trip Is a Scouting Trip

All industries have a place where the best people congregate. Be there and be thinking about recruiting talent. That's what the best CEOs (and VCs) do; they always have their talent switch turned on. They might be invited to be a keynote speaker at a convention, they might have traveled to a trade show to massage their biggest clients, they may be at a conference to troll for new clients. But one thing is for sure: they will also have one eye out for potential talent. Get to know people at other companies, shake some hands, swap some business cards—and then put them into a new section of your handheld database under "talent." When a post comes up, you'll already have a list of names. And when you call them, they will remember you. If you're a good manager, you will already be programmed to spend time at such industry events,

searching for new customers. You must now also be on the lookout
for talent.

I myself never miss a chance to do some recruiting. If I'm on a
plane and find myself sitting next to a smart, articulate executive
who lives in San Francisco or Boston or in any of the other cities
where Christian & Timbers has offices, I immediately switch into
recruiting mode. In fact, I have made it a habit to talk to everyone
who sits next to me on a plane. When I was about twenty-five, I was
on a business trip to upstate New York and feeling a bit sorry for
myself. I was in my robotics period, and I had an idea for creating
a venture firm that would invest in the automation industry. I had
even written a business plan. But I didn't have any contacts in the
venture business, and I had this terrible feeling that at my age I was
not about to meet the right people. I took some pleasure in the fact
that the seat next to me was empty and I could spread out and get
some work done. But before I could enjoy that prospect, someone
sat down—a teenager, no less. Not only was my work space gone,
but I would be sitting next to someone who was not a potential
client or job candidate. I talked to him anyway. He was an under-
graduate at Cornell, and his father, who was sitting a few rows
away, was taking him to Ithaca. I asked what his father did. "He's
in the venture business," the boy replied. "In Cleveland." He introduced us, and during a layover in Pittsburgh, we talked. John
Linseth turned out to be an entrepreneur and self-made multimil-
lionaire who was very well connected in my hometown. I told him
about my venture idea, and he suggested I talk to his other son.
"He's a lot like you—lots of ideas." I did look up his son. Steve Linseth and I started a little venture-capital firm that complemented
my infant search business by helping to generate new clients and
introducing us to other people in the venture world.

Never pass up a chance to add to your network. If you're sitting next to an executive at a basketball game and notice evidence of those Formula Five leadership skills, strike up a conversation. He might know someone you ought to hire. Headhunting at sporting events may seem a bit radical, but it works. That is exactly how we found our VP of marketing. Our CFO got to talking to someone at a baseball game.

### Don't Be Shy About Approaching People

Your first words do not have to be, "Come to work with me." There are plenty of things to talk about, particularly if you're in the same industry. Mention one of their successes, ask for some advice, raise the possibility of having lunch one day, or ask them for suggestions for a particular position. Who knows? They might even suggest themselves. In my experience, when you make a recruiting or networking call—"I'm wondering if you might know someone who could fill this job"—you get one of three responses: (1) "No, I can't help you"; (2) "Here's a name or two for you"; or (3) "Let me close my door." George W. Bush asked Dick Cheney to head his search for vice presidential possibilities. We know who emerged as the top candidate.

### Read the Trades

If someone is getting a lot of publicity in your industry, then maybe you should get to know him. Trade publications are on the lookout for the newcomers in their area. At my company, we have people who specialize in recruiting for particular industries. If they're covering telecom or software—today's hottest spaces—

they are also tracking the trades in that area; same with all the other industries we recruit in. Consider the trades as assistant talent scouts for your network.

### If Someone Has a Lot of Time to Talk to You, Hang Up

Early on in my career, I came up with a motto for myself: "Anyone who'd fly to meet me about a job disqualified himself the minute he landed." I want the kind of candidate that *I* have to chase. Same thing on the phone: winners will not have the time to talk to you. And when they do, they are brief, focused, and to the point. Those are the qualities that a headhunter looks for in an interview, and you should keep the same traits in mind when you're scouting your talent network. You do not need anyone in your pipeline with too much time on their hands.

### Take Advantage of the Natural Recruiters on Your Team

We all know someone who seems to know everyone. And just as typically, every company has someone who has an eye for local talent, someone who is always eager to attract better people to the company. I used to have a colleague who seemed unable to leave the building without running into someone he thought had what it took to be a good headhunter. His antennae were always out for the skills of a good search professional. Every company needs a natural networker like that. Never discourage your colleagues from recommending talent. Some companies even offer prizes or rewards for employee referrals.

## No Matter How Good Your Network Is, Keep Improving It

Coming up with the talent that is not on every other search firm's list is also part of my job. You have to dig into corners that no one else has thought about. Certainly that is why venture capitalists, who used to find their own CEOs, now work with headhunters, or bring headhunters in as partners. "We like to use our relationship with your firm as a competitive weapon," explained one New York VC I've worked with often. In my experience, a headhunter has to be not only persistent but proactive. You have to be open to new possibilities. For example, today I have the names of four candidates on my desk for a CEO search we're doing for a $1 billion public Internet company. Those four are the obvious candidates for the job—if I listed their names here, people in the industry would say, "Well, of course." We had gone after all the prime candidates at major media companies because our client was a media company; we also went after the best subscription people because this company is also in the subscription space. But in the last ten days, we decided to try to transcend the obvious by considering stars at various networking and other companies that have something to do with supporting the Internet—because that is what our client is all about. Suddenly, I found myself in touch with the number two guy at one of the best-known technology networking firms—a person who had turned us down on literally hundreds of searches. This job, however, caught his interest, and he was willing to talk to us. We scored because we weren't satisfied with the obvious. We expanded our network.

## PART III

# CONCLUSION

## CHAPTER 9

## It's All About Talent

I have made recruiting talent my life's work. You have to do the same. I know that sounds like hyperbole, but it is quite simply the most direct route to success in business today. Analyze the most exceptional entrepreneurs you can think of, the people who have become billionaires by the time they were into their forties— Amazon's Jeff Bezos, Intuit's Scott Cook, Sun Microsystem's Scott McNealy, Teletech's Ken Tuchman. Consider the careers of such exceptional business leaders as Bill Gates, Michael Dell, and Andy Grove, who have built hugely successful companies relatively quickly; track the success rates of legendary venture capitalists such as John Doerr and Vinod Khosla, who have launched scores of successful companies and made hundreds of millions of dollars on their investments. These people know something you do not know. After twenty years of discussing business leadership with exceptional leaders, I now know it, too: *the company with the best peo-*

*ple thrives.* The Talent Principle is behind their triumphs. And if you aspire to greatness, or if you would be satisfied with being the most successful person in your industry, or even just your department, you, too, will have to embrace the Talent Principle with almost religious fervor.

I believe in talent so strongly that I think it is a revolutionary idea capable of improving not just careers or companies but the entire economy. We love to look back at the past and point to inventions that changed the world: electricity, the telephone, the Model T, the assembly line, the airplane, and more recently the personal computer and the Internet. At the time, critics derided every one of those things as a newfangled gizmo or fad that would never last. My prediction is that a century from now, historians will point to this period in American business history as the moment when the importance of talent in business came into its own.

The problem with the Talent Principle is that it is a bit like the wind: we know it's there but we can't quite catch it or pin it down. Businesspeople are not comfortable with notions they cannot easily see or measure empirically. In the business world, we have spent our time analyzing what makes *things* tick. But business isn't just about products, or being first to market, or even innovation. Great ideas drive companies—but only for so long, and then people must do the rest. Too many companies have failed because their leadership was cruising on past successes. Entrepreneurial organizations typically run aground early because all their assets are in technology and innovation rather than in talent. But what makes *people* tick keeps resisting scientific analysis. No one has yet invented a way to scan a VP of marketing's brain on a daily basis to find out why he is more successful than the previous VP of marketing. It is only recently that economists have come to understand the contribution to the economy of "human capital." New measurements of productivity and talent's effects on it are beginning to emerge. While people like myself have been trumpeting the importance of talent in business for years, we now have the technology for proving that the Talent Principle is more than a catchy slogan for search firms lining up clients. Companies can now evaluate the difference talent makes. Studies are now being done on how to identify those who perform well in business and those who simply talk a good game. We now know how talent turned General Electric into a company worth $500 billion and why Westinghouse is just a memory. Recently, I interviewed one of Jack Welch's lieutenants who left GE to run a multibillion-dollar business for another big company. He conceded that he had not realized how much he had come to depend on the great talent around him until he went to another organization where the culture was not as committed to having the best people in every job as was the case at GE.

For many companies the Talent Principle is an elusive goal. While it is easy for me to get clients to commit to the idea that their future hangs on hiring and keeping talent, their next crisis is likely to distract them from their talent search. "I believe in the Talent Principle" is easy to say; for most companies, implementing the Talent Principle can be like climbing Everest. But whether you are making a small change in a company, transforming the entire organization, or taking it from ruin and turning it around, all you need is talent. You cannot afford to disagree with me, because surrounding yourself with talent is a strategy that will have the most positive results—short-term as well as long—of anything you can do in business. And I mean *anything*.

In this book I have tried to accomplish three things: (1) make a case for talent being the single most effective way to transform a company or a career; (2) show that talent has less to do with what you have done than with who you are—and your potential as a leader; (3) help you recognize genuine talent, get such people to work for you, and make sure they are so happy that they will never want to leave your side. My refrain has been: *Talent is the key to your success.* No matter whether you are starting your career or trying to reignite it; whether you are trying to fix some specific problems in your company or pull off a complete turnaround; whether you are trying to raise financing or invest in a new business— talent is your silver bullet. If you get the right talent quotient into your business, you can fix anything or build anything. No matter where you are in your career, if you attract other talent to your side, you will keep rising.

By reading this book, you have shown that you care about improving your career. That tells me you already have some momentum. But it can stop. In fact, momentum eventually comes to a halt in 99 percent of all careers. An elite 1 percent just seem to keep going right to the top of the pyramid. The CEOs who run the biggest and best companies in the world have something extra that fuels their success: they understand talent. Talent is not just about what you have done. Being a successful businessperson is about who you are—your honesty, integrity, and humility; it's about the innate skills of energy, drive, passion, and intellectual power. Above all, talent is about being a leader who knows how to get things done *through people.* Embracing the Talent Principle is about digging deep into your own organization to identify the exceptional performers, the people so good that everyone else will want to steal them. It is about moving outside your company to listen to your customers—to find the talent among them who can teach you about your business from the client's side, who can help you solve problems you might not even know you have.

The sooner you learn the Talent Principle, the quicker you internalize the truth that the way you attack the competition, innovate better than they do, get things to market first, increase your market share, build customer loyalty, and cut costs is with people. Great careers are also built on the Talent Principle. You cannot do it alone. You also have to keep learning how to use talent better and more productively. It is a continual contest that should begin with your first job. As an individual contributor in a company, you must attach yourself to the best people in your department. You must find a mentor. And when you are promoted to manage other employees, you must identify the best ones, cultivate the average ones, and get rid of the worst. You must build teams and make tough decisions quickly and correctly. Most important, you must have the answers to these questions: What is the overall vision? Where are we all going? Who is going to do what? What do we need in order to get it done? How are we going to make it happen? How do we keep communicating the vision? How do we keep everyone connected to the vision? And once the job is executed, good managers will hold people accountable, and they will debrief everyone to find out how to do it better next time.

That is the methodology of success. When I ask great business leaders how they get things done, this is how they all do it. In fact, this is how talented managers operate at every level of business. They take their corner vision in the company's strategy, engage the best people, keep them charged up, and achieve their goals. If you can pull all that off routinely in your position of managing managers, you soon will be a manager of people who manage managers, a company vice president or a director. You have now left 70 to 80 percent of the people you began your career with behind. Their momentum stalled because they stopped leveraging talent properly. But it is no time for gloating. For if you do not keep finding new ways to apply the Talent Principle, you will soon find yourself stuck in that vice president's office. You get to the CEO's office on the shoulders of the talent you promote and deploy.

Of course, there are other ways of looking at business—from the point of view of products, or sales, or even profits. But I would advise you to junk those viewpoints. If you think that success in business is about numbers or models, you are wrong. If you learned in business school that success in business is about things other than people, you have a lot of unlearning to do. The numbers, marketing research, business models, and everything else that business professors teach are important to success in the marketplace. But surrounding yourself with talent must be your number-one priority, or you will find yourself struggling forever—because sales, marketing, business models, and finance do not exist without people. The great CEOs never say, "Okay, what should I do to fix this marketing problem?" They say, "The way to fix this marketing problem is to get a new marketing person in here." When people walk away, the documents filled with strategies and numbers just sit there on the desk. Paperwork does not fix problems, talent does. If you have the right people in those jobs at the right time, everything else happens.

What is a great reputation but a name that rests on the talents of others? To embrace the Talent Principle is to give yourself an opportunity to create an extraordinary legacy. When people talk about you they will say, "This is a person who built organizations and got things done. This is a person who put other people's agendas first and put aside his own. This is a person I wish everyone else would be like." Whether you are a middle manager, district sales manager, general manager, CFO, or CEO of a successful company, other people will point to you as an example of the right way of doing things. Isn't that what we all say about successful people? The only thing that I am adding is that the reason they are worth pointing to is because they banked their careers and their companies on finding and keeping the best people in every job.

But you cannot just read this book. It's not enough simply to agree with me. You have to go out and do what I say. Every day of your career. I hardly ever meet anyone who argues that companies don't succeed on the strength of their people. But very few people walk the walk. Sometimes it is because they are so full of their own talent that they will not accept the idea that everyone needs help; sometimes they simply do not understand what talent really is. And sometimes it is because they themselves have never been exposed to enough talent or were never blessed with good coaching. But more often than not, companies fail to embrace the Talent Principle because they simply do not know how to pull it off—how to find talent, hire it, and keep it. There is no quick fix for talent. Unfortunately, too many people today spend all their time at quick fixes, reacting to the markets, to shareholders, to their boards. The primary route to success is working at talent, and that is a very long and tough road indeed.

I hope this book will make your journey easier.

# ACKNOWLEDGMENTS

Twenty years as a headhunter has proved to me the importance and power of talent in creating great companies. I have now learned that this same Talent Principle also applies to creating a book. I have been extremely lucky to be the beneficiary of a talented team, which has taken this book from just an idea to what you now hold in your hands. I want to go on record with my gratitude for their contributions, hard work, and support at every stage of this project.

My PR man extraordinaire, Rob Wyse, was the person who first suggested that I ought to write a book and then kept suggesting it until I took the prospect seriously. Then he introduced me to New York literary agent Jim Levine, who came up with the idea of the book I should write. Jim then connected me with the writer Edward Tivnan, who helped us fine-tune a proposal that sparked the interest of several publishing houses. I was delighted that Random

House seemed as enthusiastic about the idea as we were. Over the next year, Tivnan helped me turn what I have learned as a headhunter into a book that would help readers build their careers and their businesses. I thank him.

My gratitude also goes to Random House's editor in chief, Ann Godoff, for recognizing how important the issue of talent is to business success and for her support for this project from the beginning. I particularly want to thank my editor, Jonathan Karp, for his enthusiasm and sharp editorial eye. He made important suggestions all along the way and was never afraid to ask tough questions.

At Christian & Timbers, I want to acknowledge the efforts of the entire marketing department in helping me gather facts and background research to fortify my ideas and arguments and then work with Random House to market the book: Kelly Brooks, Lesley Cawley, Kate Clegg, Brenda Gonyea, Rebecca Lovell, Tom Loveman, and Caroline Montoya. I am also grateful to Sarah Steele, who helped me prepare speeches and other projects that became test-drives for notions that ended up in the book. My assistants Jane Christen and Martha Peta helped me juggle my schedule so that I could work on the book without taking my eye off my responsibilities to the firm and my clients. Martha also conspired with Tivnan to make sure I was available to put in the time it took to prepare the manuscript and revise it.

I also want to thank my co-CEO, Steve Mader, who has been a mentor of mine in the search business. And my brother, Adam Kohn, who proved his own talent by working his way up in the firm. Adam also keeps me aware of my shortcomings, with a smile and affection.

No headhunter can succeed without clients. The CEOs and

other top managers I have worked with have provided me the kind of education in business that no B-school could ever match. I also want to thank them for giving Christian & Timbers the opportunity to compete with the big search firms. But I particularly want to thank Lew Platt, the retired CEO of Hewlett-Packard, for hiring me to lend him a hand in his efforts to transform HP. It was my first major strategic corporate account, and I will never forget Lew for giving me the biggest break of my career.

Finally, I want to thank my mother, a writer who always encouraged me to be creative and insisted that I could accomplish anything I set my mind to. And my father, a forty-three-year veteran of the search game who taught me the business and keeps sending fine talent my way. Above all, I must thank my loving wife, Lori. It cannot be easy living with someone who spends as much time working as I do—then decides to write a book.

# INDEX

JEFFREY E. CHRISTIAN is one of the world's top headhunters. As founder and CEO of Christian & Timbers, the firm that has connected thousands of executives with brilliant careers, Christian counsels many of the nation's top CEOs on strategies for how to win the war for talent. He has also created C&T Access Ventures, a venture capital fund that invests in promising young companies. For two straight years, Christian has been named to the Forbes "Midas List" as one of the top fifty deal makers in technology.

**ABOUT THE TYPE**

This book was set in Minion, a 1990 Adobe Originals typeface by Robert Slimbach. Minion is inspired by classical, old-style type-faces of the late Renaissance, a period of elegant, beautiful, and highly readable type designs. Created primarily for text setting, Minion combines the aesthetic and functional qualities that make text type highly readable with the versatility of digital technology.